Humility

by Andrew Murray

with

The Blood of the Lamb the Conquering Weapon

by Charles H. Spurgeon

HeavenReigns.com

Humility
by Andrew Murray

Rendered into contemporary English

© 2003 HeavenReigns.com

ଔ

The Blood of the Lamb, the Conquering Weapon
by Charles H. Spurgeon

Rendered into contemporary English

© 2008 HeavenReigns.com

For more encouragement in your walk with Jesus, we invite you to read and listen to the free material on HeavenReigns.com and JesusLifeTogether.com.

ISBN 978-0-9849436-2-3

"May I never boast except in the cross of our Lord Jesus Christ, through which the world has been crucified to me, and I to the world."

Saul of Tarsus—and you?

Contents

Humility

The Blood of the Lamb, the Conquering Weapon

Preface: Why Focus on Humility?

There are three things that should motivate me to be humble. *Humility is the only normal way for me to live as a man.* This healthy desire to take a rightful place under God moves the angels in heaven, just as it did Adam and Eve when they were freshly created and Jesus when he lived as the carpenter from Galilee. Humility also gives me hope as a sinner. It appeals to us humans in our fallen condition and points out the only way to return to our right place in God's creation. *Finally, humility strengthens me as a saint.* Grace teaches us that as we lose ourselves in the overwhelming greatness of God's love, humility before Him is caught up in everlasting blessedness and worship.

Sadly, Christians have focused almost all of their attention on that second motive, on why sinners need to humble themselves. Some people have even gone so far as to say that it's a good thing for Christians to keep on sinning, to keep them humble. How foolish, and how sad! Others have thought that the secret of humility is to walk around with a dark cloud of condemnation hanging over your head. These misunderstandings have robbed God's children of their inheritance. Too many of us don't realize how wonderful and natural it is to become nothing, so that Jesus can be our All in All! We haven't been taught that it isn't *sin* that humbles us the most, but *grace.* Who is it that will bow down the lowest at Jesus' feet? It is the men and women whom He has led out of their sinfulness and filled with awe at their glorious God as their Creator and Redeemer.

In the thoughts that follow I have chosen to focus attention almost exclusively on the humility that is fitting for redeemed people. I assume that most of you already understand that a sinner should be humble. But even more importantly, I believe that if you are to experience Jesus in His Fullness, you need to understand thoroughly your own need for humility. If Jesus is your example, your pattern, you need to know what motivated *Him* to be humble. If we are going to take our stand with Jesus, it needs to be on the ground *He's* standing on. That's where we'll grow to become more like Him. If we are going to become humble before God and our fellow man—if humility is to become our *joy*—we can't just think that humility is a sense of shame for our sin. We also have to understand it separate and apart from all sin as a *covering with the beauty and blessedness of heaven and of Jesus Himself.*

Just as Jesus found His glory in taking the form of a servant, He has also told us, "The greatest among you must be a servant" (Matt. 23:11). He simply was teaching us the truth. Nothing is so wonderful and godly as being the servant and helper of all! The faithful servant who recognizes his or her position finds a real pleasure in meeting the needs and desires of the Master or His guests. When we see that humility is something far deeper than just feeling sorry for sin and accept it as taking part in the life and heart of Jesus, we will begin to see it as our true nobility. We will begin to see that being servants of all is the highest fulfillment of our destiny, as human beings created in the image of God.

When I look at my own experience, along with that of other Christians I have known throughout the world, I am amazed how little humility is sought after as the distinguishing feature of being Jesus' disciple. In the activities of daily life in the home and with others, and in the more special fellowship with Christians as we work for Jesus, there is far too much evidence that humility is not held up as the highest character trait to seek after. People don't seem to realize that humility is the only root that other good character traits can grow out of. It is the one indispensable condition of true fellowship with Jesus. Unfortunately, people looking for a deeper holiness have not always pursued it with increased humility. Test your heart to see whether meekness and lowliness are the main ways you are seeking to follow the meek, humble Lamb of God!

1. Humility: The Glory of God's Creation

The twenty-four elders fall down and worship the One who lives forever and ever. And they lay their crowns before the throne and say, "You are worthy, O Lord our God, to receive glory and honor and power. For You created everything, and it is for Your pleasure that they exist and were created." (Rev. 4:10-11)

God wanted one thing when He created the universe: to show in it the glory of His love, wisdom, and power. He meant for human beings to share in His perfection and blessedness as part of that creation. God wanted to reveal Himself in and through created beings by filling them to the brim with His own goodness and glory. But God did not give Adam and Eve some *independent* goodness for them claim as their own apart from Him. No way!

God is ever living, ever present, and ever active. He upholds all things with His powerful Word. All things exist in Him. So the relationship of man to God could only be through continual, absolute, total dependence. God created by His power, and He must hold His creation together by that same power. We only have to look back to our origin to realize we owe everything to God. Our main goal, our highest good, and our only happiness—now and forever—is to offer ourselves to God as empty vessels that He can fill, to show His power and goodness.

God doesn't give us life once and for all, then leave. He gives us life moment by moment, with a constant working of His mighty power. Humility—the place of total dependence on God—is our primary duty and highest good. That's just how the universe is put together!

So pride—the loss of this humility—is the root of every sin and evil. When did the devil and his angels start down that road of disobedience that led to them being cast down from the light of heaven into outer darkness? It was when they began to be focused on themselves. When the serpent injected the venom of his pride—the desire to be like God—into Adam and Eve, they, too, fell from the special place God had made for them. They dove headlong into all of the wretchedness you see their descendants in now. In all of heaven and earth, pride and exalting yourself are the gate to hell—and its greatest curse.

It is obvious, then, that nothing can be right again until our lost humility is restored. That humility is the original and only true relationship a human being can have with God. Jesus came to bring humility back to earth, to make us sharers in it, and by it to save us. In heaven, He humbled Himself to become a man. The humility we see in Him, he possessed in Heaven. Humility brought Jesus, and Jesus brought humility, down to earth. Once He was here, "He obediently humbled Himself even further by dying" (Phil. 2:8). His humility gave His death its value, and so became our redemption. Now the salvation He offers us is nothing less than being joined to His life and death, His character and spirit. His own humility is the foundation of His relationship with the Father and His work to redeem us. He took our place and fulfilled our destiny by His life of perfect humility. His humility is our salvation. His salvation is our humility.

If our salvation is real, our lives should be stamped with the mark of being delivered from sin and restored to our place as God's vessels. Our whole relationship to God and to other people must be marked by humility, through and through. Otherwise, how could we live in God's presence, experiencing His love and the power of His Spirit? Without taking our place of dependence, we can't have a *lasting* faith or love or joy or strength. Life will be full of ups and downs. Humility is the only soil where Christ-like character can take root. A lack of humility is the only explanation you need for every flaw and failure you have. Humility is not one of many good character traits; it is the root of all of them, because it places us in the right relationship with God and frees Him up to do all that He desires. God gave us the ability to think logically for a reason. If we can only see our absolute need for His command that we be humble, we will *want* to obey, with all our minds. But God's people have not really understood His call to humility. Our minds have been dull to its importance.

Humility is not a *thing* we bring to God. It is also not a *thing* God gives to us. It is simply the *realization of what nothings we really are, when we truly see how God is Everything, and when we clear out room in our hearts so that He can be everything for us*. We have to understand that this realization is the only noble thing we can every really think or do. We must make a choice, with our wills, minds, and emotions, to become empty vessels that God can fill with His life and glory. Then we will see that humility is simply acknowledging the truth about who we are and yielding to God His rightful place.

For true disciples, who are pursuing holiness, humility should be the number one evidence of their righteousness. But how rare this humility on our planet today! It may be that the teaching and example of those who are supposed to be leaders in God's House has never reflected the emphasis He gives humility. This truth has been almost forgotten: although sin is a powerful motive for humility, there is a stronger one. This motive makes the angels in heaven and the Son of God Himself so humble. Here it is: the core of man's relationship to God, the secret to blessing, is the humility and nothingness that leaves God free to be All.

Many Christians are probably just like me. We knew the Lord a long time without realizing that meekness and lowliness of heart should be the distinguishing feature of the disciple, as they were of the Master. Humility doesn't just "happen." We have to want it. It requires faith, prayer, and practice. As we lean into God's Word, we will see that Jesus gave His disciples clear and frequent teaching on this point. We will also see how slow they were to understand it.

From the start, let's admit that nothing comes quite so naturally to us—and nothing is so hidden in our blind spots—as pride. That's why it is so dangerous. Let's realize that nothing but a determined and persevering seeking of God will open our eyes to see how lacking we are in humility and how feeble we are in obtaining it! Let's fix our eyes on Jesus until our souls are filled with love and admiration for His humility. And let's believe that, when we are broken down under a sense of our pride and realize our inability to get rid of it, that Jesus Christ Himself will give us this grace as a part of His wonderful Life within us.

2. Humility: The Secret of Redemption

Your attitude should be the same that Christ Jesus had. Though He was God, He did not demand and cling to His rights as God. He made Himself nothing; He took the humble position of a slave and appeared in human form. And in human form He obediently humbled Himself even further by dying a criminal's death on a cross. Because of this, God raised Him up to the heights of heaven and gave Him a name that is above every other name. (Phil. 2:5-9)

A tree grows from its own root. Its whole existence, the tree lives with the same life that was in the seed that produced it. That truth can help us see *why* we need to be redeemed and *how* God has met that need.

The devil was thrown down from heaven because of his pride. His whole character *is* pride. When he hissed his words of temptation into Eve's ear, his words dripped with the venom of hell. And when she listened and yielded her heart and will to the desire to be like God, knowing good and evil for herself, that venom entered her spiritual bloodstream and poisoned her life. Gone forever was the wonderful humility and dependence on God that would have guaranteed the everlasting happiness of the human race. Instead, human life became corrupted with the most terrible of all sin and curses, the poison of the devil's own pride.

All of the wretchedness the world has seen began with that curse. Hellish pride—either our own or someone else's—is responsible for all the misery we've experienced. All war and bloodshed among nations, all selfishness and suffering, all ambition and jealousy, every broken heart and bitter life, are the results of this same wicked pride.

It is because of pride that we need to be redeemed. If we are to grasp how desperately we need Jesus, we must see the terrible power that pride has over us.

The power that Satan brought from hell and injected into human life is working daily—hourly—with incredible force throughout the world. People suffer from it. They fear it, fight against it, and try to run away from it. But they still don't know where it comes from or why it is so strong. No wonder they have no clue about how to overcome it!

Pride's power is in the spiritual realm, both inside and outside us. We need to confess it, hate it, and realize its satanic origin. Seeing pride for what it is may cause us to despair of ever overcoming it and removing it from our hearts. But it will also drive us to discover the supernatural power that is our only hope—the redemption of the Lamb of God. Our hopeless struggle against self and pride may seem even more hopeless when we think of the power of darkness that is against us. But eventually we will better realize and accept the power and life are offered to us—the humility of heaven, brought into our hearts by the Lamb of God to cast out the devil and his pride.

If we need to look at Adam and Eve's sin to understand the power of the sin that's inside us, how much more do we need to know the power of the Second Adam, Jesus. He offers us a life of humility that is even more real and lasting and powerful than our pride. Our life is from and in Christ. We are to "let our roots grow down into Him," for "we grow only as we get our nourishment and strength from God" (Col. 2:7, 19).

The life of God, which entered the human race when Jesus was born, is the root where we must stand and grow. The same power that worked in Jesus, from the manger to the empty tomb, can work daily in us. Do you know what our main need is? It is to know and trust that the life that has been revealed in Christ is now *our* life. His life is waiting only for our permission to gain possession and mastery over our whole being.

We need to know Christ! We must see Him clearly. We especially need a revelation of the root of His character as our Redeemer:

His humility. What did Jesus' birth mean, except that with heavenly humility He was emptying Himself and becoming one of us? What was His life on earth about, if it wasn't taking the form of a servant? What was the cross, other than the most humble act the universe has ever witnessed? "He obediently humbled Himself even further by dying a criminal's death on a cross." And what was Jesus' ascension to God's throne, except humility crowned with glory? "God raised Him up to the heights of heaven and gave Him a name that is above every other name."

In heaven, where Jesus was with the Father, in His birth, in His life, in His death, and on His throne, everything was and is humility. Christ is the humility of God embodied in human nature. He is eternal love humbling itself, clothing itself with meekness and gentleness, to win and serve and save us. Love is what makes God the servant of all, and humility is what makes Jesus who He is. Even on the throne, He is the meek and lowly Lamb of God.

Humility is the root of the tree. You can tell it by looking at every branch and leaf and fruit. If the secret of Jesus' life and death is humility, then the health and strength of our own spiritual lives will completely depend on our making humility our top priority, too. We must make humility the thing we admire about Him most, the main thing we ask of Him, and the one thing we see that we can't live without.

Is it any wonder that the so-called "Christian life" is so often weak and fruitless, if the root of the Christ-life is neglected? Should we be surprised that the joy of salvation is so little felt, when the place where Jesus found it—the place of lowliness—is so little searched for? We must seek a humility that will settle for nothing less than dying to self. We must decide to give up trying to get men to honor us and seek the honor that comes only from God. We must learn to count ourselves as nothing so that God may be everything, that Jesus alone will be lifted up. Until we make humility our main joy and welcome it at any price, there is very little hope of a faith that will overcome the world.

How much that is called by Jesus' name really demonstrates this humility? That about the lack of love, the indifference towards others' needs, the sharp and critical judgment of others that we are so quick to excuse. Think of the temper and irritation, the bitterness and loneliness that have their root in pride. Pride only seeks itself.

Devilish pride creeps in almost everywhere. What would happen if believers were to become permanently guided by the humility of Jesus? Oh, for the meekness of Jesus in myself and in everyone around me! We must honestly set our hearts on Jesus' humility, and how far we fall short of it. Only then will we begin to feel what Christ and His salvation really are.

Do you believe in Jesus? Then study His humility! It is the secret, the hidden root of your redemption. Sink down into it more deeply day by day. Believe with your whole heart that Christ—God's gift to us—will work in us, making us what the Father wants us to be.

3. Humility in the Life of Jesus

Normally the master sits at the table and is served by his servants. But not here! For I am your servant (Luke 22:27).

John's gospel opens a window to the inner life of Jesus. Often Jesus spoke of His relationship with His Father. He revealed the motives that guided Him. He shared the heart behind what He did. Although the word "humble" doesn't appear in John, Jesus' humility is revealed there like nowhere else in Scripture.

We have already defined humility as a person's simple consent to let God be everything—a surrender to His purposes. In Jesus we will see the perfect example of humility. Both as the Son of God in heaven and the Son of Man on earth, he took the place of complete submission. He gave God the honor and the glory that are due Him. He lived what He taught: "The humble will be honored." As the Scriptures say, "He obediently humbled Himself...because of this, God raised Him up to the heights of heaven."

Listen to these words from John's gospel where Jesus speaks of His relationship with His Father. Notice how often He uses the words "not" and "nothing" of Himself. The "not I" that Paul uses to speak of his own relationship to Christ is the same heart Jesus expresses when He speaks of His relationship with the Father.

- "The Son can do *nothing* by Himself" (John 5:19).

- "I do *nothing* without consulting the Father. I judge as I am told. And My judgment is absolutely just, because it is according to the will of God who sent Me; it is *not* merely My own" (John 5:30).

- "For I have come down from heaven to do the will of God who sent Me, *not* to do what I want" (John 6:38).

- "I'm *not* teaching My own ideas, but those of God who sent Me" (John 7:16).

- "I do *nothing* on My own, but I speak what the Father has taught Me" (John 8:28).

- "I am *not* here on My own, but He sent Me" (John 8:42).

- "I have *no* wish to glorify Myself" (John 8:50).

- "The words I say are *not* My own, but the Father who lives in Me does His work through Me" (John 14:10).

- "And remember, My words are *not* My own. This message is from the Father who sent Me" (John 14:24).

These words expose the deepest roots of Christ's life and work. They show why Almighty God could perform His mighty work of redemption through Him. They demonstrate how important it was to Jesus to have the right heart towards His Father. And they teach us the inner character of that Life that came to save us and *now* can live *in* us.

Jesus became nothing, so that the Father could be *everything*. He submitted His strength and will completely so that the Father could work in Him. What did Jesus have to say about His own power, His own will, and His own glory, about His whole mission with all His works and teaching? "It is not I; I am nothing; I have given Myself to the Father to work. I am nothing. The Father is everything."

Christ found this life of complete self-surrender, of absolute submission and dependence on God's will, to be perfect peace and joy. He lost nothing by giving everything to God! The Father honored Jesus' trust and did everything for Him, then raised Him up to His own right hand in glory. And because Christ humbled Himself before God in that way, and because God was always near Him, He found it possible to humble Himself before men, too. He was able to be Servant of all. Jesus' humility was simply surrender of Himself to God. He let the Father do in Him whatever He wanted. It didn't matter what people around Him said of Him or did to Him.

It is with this heart and attitude that Christ's redemption is powerful and effective. It is so that *we* will have this same Spirit that we have been allowed to share in Christ. When Jesus calls us to deny ourselves and follow Him, this is what He means: that we admit that self has no value except as an empty vessel for God to fill. The claim of self to be or do anything must not be allowed for one moment. More than anything else, humility is what becoming like Jesus is all about. We are to be and do nothing by ourselves so that God may be All.

In Jesus we discover what humility means. It is because we don't understand or seek after it that our own humility is so shallow and feeble. We need to learn from Jesus how He is so meek and humble in heart. He teaches us where true humility finds its strength—in the knowledge that only God is good, and that our place is to yield to Him in perfect submission and dependence. We must agree to be and do nothing of ourselves. This Life is what Jesus came to show us and give us—a Life in God that comes from death to sin and self.

Are you feeling that this Life is too far beyond you, that you could never reach it? Then let that realization drive you to seek the answer in Him. Only Jesus, living inside of us, can live this life of humility in us. If we long for it, let us ask Jesus for His secret. That secret—which is meant for every child of God to know—is that Jesus lived His life as a vessel, a channel through whom the Living God could show the riches of His wisdom, power, and goodness. The energy behind all spiritual growth and all faith and genuine worship comes from a conviction that all that we have comes from God. Then we will bow in deepest humility to wait on Him for it.

For Jesus, humility wasn't just some temporary emotion that He felt when He thought about His Father. It was the very Spirit of His whole life. That's why He could be just as humble with people as He was with His Father. He considered Himself only a Servant of God, sent for God's purposes to the men and women

He had created and loved. It was very natural, then, that He thought of Himself as a servant through whom the Father could do His work of love. Jesus never thought for a moment of seeking His own honor or asserting His own power to prove anything about Himself. His whole Spirit was that of a life yielded to God so that He could work through it. It is not until Christians open their hearts to this revelation of Jesus' humility that we will start feeling the empty space in our own hearts—the space that humility was meant to fill. When we realize that humility is the only true relationship to the Father, we will hurt over our lack of reality with God. Whatever we may be satisfied with about our "Christian life" must be set aside as nothing until we find Jesus' humility.

Brother or sister, are you clothed with humility? Ask your daily life. Ask Jesus. Ask your friends. Ask the world. And begin to praise God that in Jesus you have a Way to a heavenly humility that you have barely understood and a blessing that you've never really tasted before.

4. Humility in the Teaching of Jesus

"Let Me teach you, because I am humble and gentle, and you will find rest for your souls" (Matt. 11:29).

"Whoever wants to be first must become your slave. For even I, the Son of Man, came here not to be served but to serve others, and to give My life as a ransom for many" (Matt. 20:27-28).

Jesus opened His heart to us, and when we looked inside, we found a wonderful humility there. Now let's listen to His teaching. Let's learn what He has to say about humility and what His expectations are of His disciples. I am going to do little more than quote some of His teachings, but I trust you to discover what they should mean to you and to press the seeds down deeply in your own heart.

1. Look at how Jesus started His season of public teaching. When He called His disciples to Him on the mountainside, He began: *"God blesses those who realize their need for Him, for the Kingdom of Heaven is given to them...God blesses those who are gentle and lowly, for the whole earth will belong to them"* (Matt. 5:3,5). The very first words of Jesus' proclamation of the Kingdom of Heaven on earth were meant to reveal the open gate where we can enter in. The poor in spirit, who have nothing in themselves, can receive the Kingdom. The meek, who seek nothing for themselves, can inherit the whole planet. The blessings of heaven and earth are for the lowly. For a life of blessing in both the seen and unseen realms, humility is the secret.

2. *"Let Me teach you, because I am humble and gentle, and you will find rest for your souls"* (Matt. 11:29). Jesus offers Himself as our Teacher. He tells us the Spirit we will find in Him as Teacher, and offers us the amazing privilege of learning and receiving that Spirit from Him! Meekness and

lowliness are what He offers; in them, we will find perfect rest for our souls. Humility is to be our deliverance.

3. The disciples had been arguing about who would be greatest in the Kingdom. To settle the matter once and for all, they agreed to go to the Master (Luke 9:46; Matt. 18:3). How startled they must have felt when He set a child in their midst and said, *"Anyone who becomes as humble as this little child is the greatest in the Kingdom of Heaven."* It is a question with far-reaching implications. What will be the most valued personal characteristic in God's holy nation on earth? No one but Jesus would have guessed the answer. The highest glory of heaven, the genuine mark of having heaven in your heart, is humility. God esteems it above all else. *"Whoever is least among you is the greatest"* (Luke 9:48).

4. The sons of Zebedee had asked Jesus for the most important places in the Kingdom, at His right and His left. Jesus said that they were not His to give, but the Father's, who would give them to those for whom He had prepared them. They must not look or ask for those places. Instead, they should think about the cup and baptism of humiliation that He would face. Then He added, *"Whoever wants to be first must become your slave. For even I, the Son of Man, came here not to be served but to serve others, and to give My life as a ransom for many."* Humility was the character of Jesus in the heavenlies. It will also be the one standard of glory in Heaven. The place nearest to God is also the lowliest. Jesus promises the prime position in His Kingdom to the humblest.

5. Once Jesus spoke to the crowds and to the disciples about the Pharisees and their love of positions of honor. He said again, *"The greatest among you must be a servant"* (Matt. 23:11). Genuine humble service, without thought of reward, is the only "ladder to success" in God's Kingdom.

6. At a Pharisee's house, Jesus told the parable of the guest who would be invited to take a better place at the banquet

and added, *"For the proud will be humbled, but the humble will be honored"* (Luke 14:11). His demand is unchangeable; there is no other way. Only people who choose to humble themselves will be honored.

7. After telling the story of the Pharisee and the tax collector, Jesus said again, *"For the proud will be humbled, but the humble will be honored"* (Luke 18:14). In the temple in the presence and worship of God, everything is worthless that isn't full of a deep, true humility toward God and men.

8. When Jesus washed the disciples feet, He said, *"And since I, the Lord and Teacher, have washed your feet, you ought to wash each other's feet"* (John 13:14). The authority of Jesus' command, example, and thought makes humility the first and most essential condition of true discipleship.

9. At their last Passover meal with their Master, the disciples were still arguing among themselves about who was the greatest. Jesus cut the debate short: *"In this world the kings and great men order their people around, and yet they are called 'friends of the people.' But among you, those who are the greatest should take the lowest rank, and the leader should be like a servant…For I am your servant"* (Luke 22:25-27). The path where Jesus walked—and opened a way for us to walk—is the way of humility that always makes me the servant of all. That humility was the power and Spirit in which He brought salvation, and the same humility is what He saves us *for*.

How little this humility is taught. How little it is lived! How little the *lack* of it is felt or confessed. I'm not saying that no one ever makes *any* progress towards Christ-likeness in this area. But I am saying that too few people think to make humility a goal that they desire and pray for. How little the world has seen it! How little it has been seen even in the "inner circles" of Christianity.

"Whoever wants to be first must become your slave." God wants us to believe that Jesus meant what He said! We can imagine what it would take to be a faithful servant or slave in the literal sense—devotion to the master's interests, thoughtful efforts to please him, delight in his prosperity and honor and happiness. A few men and women have had that attitude, and to them the name of "servant" has been something to glory in.

To many of us it has been a new joy in our walk with Jesus to know that we can yield ourselves as servants, as slaves to God. We have discovered that service to Him is true freedom—the freedom from sin and self. We need now to learn another lesson. Jesus also calls us to be servants of one another. If we accept this command willingly it, too, will be delight to obey. It will mean a new and fuller freedom from sin and self. At first this service may seem hard, but that's only because of lingering pride that still considers itself to *be* something.

We can learn that to be *nothing* before God is our glory, Jesus' Spirit, and Heaven's joy. Then we will welcome with our whole hearts the discipline that comes our way when serving the unlovable. When our own hearts are set on this kind of service, every word Jesus spoke about humility will take on new life for us. No position will seem too low. No stooping will be too deep and no service too humble or too hard to endure, if only we can know the fellowship of the One who said, "For I am your servant."

Brothers and sisters, the path to the "higher life" is down, lower down! Jesus was always faithful to remind His disciples of that fact whenever they were thinking about greatness in the Kingdom, of sitting at His right or left hand. Don't seek or ask for honor; that's God's responsibility. See to it that you humble yourself and take no place before God or man except that of a servant. Your responsibility is humble service. Let that also be your one goal and prayer. God is faithful. Just as water always runs to the lowest place, so the moment God finds people humble and empty, His Glory and Power will flow into them to lift them up and bless them. Humble yourself. That's your part. Honoring us—that's God's part. By His mighty power and great love He will do it.

People sometimes talk as if humility and meekness will rob us of everything bold and admirable and worthwhile. Oh, that all would believe that humility is what *God* admires! If only we would understand that humility is the royal attitude of the King of Heaven, that it is Godlike to humble yourself and become the servant of all! That path is the only one leading to the joy and glory of Christ's presence inside us and His power resting on us.

Jesus, the meek and lowly One, calls us to learn from Him the path to God. Let us absorb the words we have been reading until our hearts are filled with the thought: My one need is humility. And let us believe that what Jesus shows, He also gives. What He is, He can impart. As the meek and lowly One, He will come in and live in the longing heart.

5. Humility in the Disciples of Jesus

"But among you, those who are the greatest should take the lowest rank, and the leader should be like a servant" (Luke 22:26).

We have looked at humility in the person and teaching of Jesus. Let's now see if we can find evidence for it in the circle of His hand-picked companions—the twelve. It we instead discover a *lack* of humility in them, then the contrast between Christ and men will be that much clearer. We'll appreciate even more the dramatic change that Pentecost produced in them. It will prove how real our participation can be in the perfect victory of Jesus' humility over the pride that the devil injected into man.

From the words of Jesus, we have already seen that the disciples demonstrated how spiritually bankrupt they were when it came to humility. Early on, it seems, they began a long running argument about which of them was the greatest. This dispute seems to have reached a new low when James and John put their mother up to requesting the places of honor—at the left and right hands of the throne—for her sons. Finally, during their last meal with Jesus before the cross, the squabble about which of them was "number one" erupted again.

Of course the disciples had their moments when one of them would genuinely humble himself before his Master. When he first met Jesus, Peter had enough sense to cry out, "Oh, Lord, please leave me—I'm too much of a sinner to be around you." All of the disciples had fallen to their knees and worshiped Jesus when He calmed the storm. But those sporadic moments of humility only serve to make their habitual pride that much more obvious. Their true colors were shown in the natural and spontaneous outbreaks of self-life in them. If we consider these men, they can teach us several critically important lessons.

First, we can see how much there can be of a very zealous and active Christianity while humility is still sadly lacking. Surely the twelve are "exhibit A." They had a sincere, passionate attachment to Jesus. They had forsaken everything for Him. The Father had revealed to them that Jesus was the Christ of God. They believed in Him, loved Him, and obeyed Him. When others turned away, they clung to Him. They were ready to die with Him. But deeper down than all their sincerity and good intentions lay a dark power. They were hardly aware of how hideous it was or that it even existed. But this power had to be killed and thrown out before they could serve as witnesses that Jesus is able to save sinners.

Things haven't changed much in 2000 years. We find many professing Christians—including those who would consider themselves "ministers," "evangelists," "missionaries," "teachers," or "full-time workers"—who seem to possess many Spiritual gifts, yet lack humility. There are people who seemingly are channels of blessing to millions, but who demonstrate, when the time of testing comes or when light shines on their lives that humility is hardly to be found in their characters. These sad examples confirm the fact that humility is the greatest and highest characteristic a person can have. It is difficult to attain, and we can't be satisfied with any less than a diligent effort to seek it. Humility is a grace that only comes with power, when the Christ is formed in us.

Secondly, we can see how weak all external teaching and personal striving is to overcome pride and produce a meek, lowly heart. For three years the disciples had been under apprenticeship to Jesus Christ. He let them know His main curriculum: "Let me teach you, because I am humble and gentle" (Matthew 11:29). Time after time He had spoken to them, to the Pharisees, and to the crowds that humility was the only path to the glory of God. He had not only lived His life before them as the Lamb of God in divine humility, He had openly shared His "secret ambition" with them. "For even I, the Son of Man, came here not to be served but to serve others, and to give my life as a ransom for many" (Mark 10:45). "For I am your servant" (Luke 22:27).

Jesus had washed their feet and told them they were to follow His example. And yet every last one of them had learned so little. At their last meal with Him, that argument was still brewing. No doubt they had tried to learn His lessons and had made up their minds that they wouldn't disappoint Him again. But it was no use! Like them, we must learn that much-needed lesson that outward teaching, even from Jesus Himself, cannot cast out the devil of pride. No arguments can convince pride away. No appreciation of humility can create it where it doesn't exist. No resolve is sincere enough to change a person's heart. When satan casts out satan, it is only to enter again in a stronger but more hidden power! Nothing can make a lasting difference, unless a new heart, with Christlike humility, takes the place of the old. It takes a miracle.

Thirdly, it is only by the indwelling of Christ in His humility that we can become humble. We didn't create pride. We can't create humility, either. Pride belongs to us, and we belong to it, because it is who we are—our very nature. Humility must be ours in the same way. It must be our very self, our very nature. The promise is, "as people sinned more and more, God's wonderful kindness became more abundant" (Romans 5:20). All Jesus' teaching of the twelve, and all their effort, were the necessary preparation for His entering into them with power. He had taught them to desire something. Now He had to *give* it to them and *be* it for them.

In His death, Jesus destroyed the power of the devil. He put away sin and accomplished an eternal redemption. In His resurrection, He received from the Father a completely new Life. It was the life of a man in the power of God, able to touch men's hearts, to enter and renew and fill their lives with power. In His ascension, Jesus received the Spirit of the Father, through whom He could accomplish what He could not have done had He stayed physically present on earth. He was able to make Himself one with those He loved, and actually live their lives for them. Then they could live before the Father in a humility like His, because it was He Himself who lived and breathed in them. And on Pentecost, He came and took possession of them.

The work of getting them ready, of awakening a desire and hope in them through His teaching, was completed with a powerful transformation through the Spirit. The lives and letters of James and Peter and John testify that everything had changed for them. The Spirit of the meek and humble Jesus truly had possession of them.

I am sure that those who hear these words find themselves in many different places spiritually. Some may not have given their pride much thought. The immense importance of this subject just may now be starting to sink in. Others may be living in condemnation. They have tried to change their pride with sincere striving, but have suffered one discouraging failure after another. Still others may testify joyfully of the spiritual blessing and power they have received in many areas, but the people close to them can testify with a good deal less joy that the power to be humble isn't one of those areas. And others may be able to say that the Lord has given them deliverance and victory here, too. He has taught them how much they still need and may expect out of the fullness of Christ.

Wherever you are personally, I urge you to seek a deeper conviction of the unique place humility holds in becoming like Jesus. We have to understand the utter impossibility of the church or the individual believer to become what Jesus wants them to be, as long as His humility is not recognized as His greatest glory, His unchanging command, and our deepest blessing. Let's deeply consider how "mature" the disciples seemed to be when humility was lacking from their characters. Let's pray to God that other gifts won't satisfy us. May we never forget that the absence of humility is the secret reason why the power of God cannot work in us. It is only when we, like the Son, truly know and show that we can do nothing of ourselves, that God will do all.

It is when the truth of "Christ in you, the hope of glory" becomes true in the experience of believers that the Church will put on her beautiful garments and humility will be seen in her members as the beauty of holiness.

6. Humility in Daily Life

"If someone says, 'I love God,' but hates a Christian brother or sister, that person is a liar; for if we don't love people we can see, how can we love God, whom we have not seen?" (1 John 4:20).

Here's a sobering thought: God measures our love for Him by the love we show our brothers and sisters in every day fellowship with them. It is a serious thing to realize that our love for God just isn't genuine if it fails the test of daily life with our fellow human beings.

The same thing is true with humility. It is easy to think we humble ourselves before God. But humility before people is the only real proof that our humility before God is more than just a figment of our imagination. It is the only true evidence that humility has made a home in our hearts and become our nature. How can we know that we, like Christ, have made ourselves of no reputation? By the reality check of daily life. When in God's presence humility has become more than just a feeling we have when we think about Him or pray, but instead the very Spirit of our lives, it will show itself in the way we treat our brothers and sisters.

This lesson is crucial. The only humility that really belongs to us is not what we try to show before God in prayer, but what we carry with us and live out when we get up off our knees. The insignificance of daily life is the test of eternity. It proves what Spirit really possesses us. It is in our unguarded moments when we show who we really are. To know the humble man, you have to follow him around and watch his daily life.

Isn't that lesson exactly what Jesus taught? His great teachings about humility came when He saw the disciples arguing about who was greatest or the Pharisees competing for the place of honor at banquets and in synagogues. He taught again after

He had given them an example by washing their feet. Humility before God is nothing if it isn't proved by humility before men.

Paul of course taught the same practical lesson. To the Romans, he wrote: "Love each other with genuine affection and take delight in honoring each other...Live in harmony with each other. Don't try to act important, but enjoy the company of ordinary people. And don't think you know it all!" (Romans 12:10,16) To the Corinthians, he said: "Love is not jealous or boastful or proud or rude. Love does not demand its own way" (1 Corinthians 13:4-5). There is no love except what grows from the root of humility! To the Galatians, Paul wrote: "For you have been called to freedom...freedom to serve one another in love...Let us not become conceited, or irritate one another, or be jealous of one another" (Galatians 5:13,26). To the Ephesians, right after those three wonderful chapters about living in Heavenly Realms, he said, "Be humble and gentle. Be patient with each other" (Ephesians 4:2). "And further, you will submit to one another out of reverence for Christ" (Ephesians 5:21). To the Philippians, Paul wrote: "Make me truly happy by agreeing wholeheartedly with each other, loving one another, and working together with one heart and purpose. Don't be selfish; don't live to make a good impression on others. Be humble, thinking of others as better than yourself...Your attitude should be the same as that Christ Jesus had...He made Himself nothing; He took the humble position of a slave and appeared in human form. And in human form He obediently humbled Himself even further by dying a criminal's death on the cross" (Philippians 2:3,5,7-8). Finally, to the Colossians, Paul said, "You must clothe yourselves with tenderhearted mercy, kindness, humility, gentleness, and patience" (Colossians 3:12). It is in our relationships, in the way we treat each other, that our true meekness of mind and humility of heart are visible. Our humility before God has no value unless it prepares us to show the humility of Jesus to our fellow men. Let us be diligent about humility in our daily lives in light of these words!

The humble person tries at all times to follow the rule, *"Take delight in honoring each other, serve one another in love, think of others as better than yourself, and submit to one another."* Maybe you are wondering, how can I count others better than myself if I see them far below me in wisdom or holiness, in natural ability or spiritual gifts? The question just shows how little we understand what humility of mind really means. True meekness comes when we see, in the light of God, that we are nothing and agree that our lives must not be our own—so God can be all. When you can say, "I have lost myself in finding You, Lord," you won't be comparing yourself to others at all. You will have given up thinking about yourself in God's presence. You will greet your fellow human being with the realization that you yourself are nothing. You won't be trying to get anything out of it for yourself. You will be God's servant and for His sake the servant of all. A faithful servant may be wiser than his master and still keep to the true spirit and position of a servant. The humble man looks at every child of God—even the weakest and unworthiest—and honors him as the King's son. The Spirit of the One who washes feet will make it a joy for us to be the least, to serve others in love.

The humble man or woman feels no jealousy or envy. Humble people can praise God when others are blessed instead of them. They are unshaken when others are praised and they themselves are forgotten. In God's presence they have learned, like Paul, to say, "I am nothing at all" (2 Corinthians 12:11). They have received the Spirit of Jesus, who refused to chase after recognition or honor.

Life on earth means that we will experience temptations to be impatient or irritable, to think resentfully or speak harshly. People around us will make mistakes. They will even sin against us. When humble people face that kind of test, they will bring up from their hearts a law that is written there: "You must bear with each other's faults and forgive the person who offends you. Remember, the Lord forgave you, so you must forgive others" (Colossians 3:13). They have learned that in putting on the Lord Jesus they have "clothed themselves with tenderhearted mercy, kindness, humility, gentleness, and patience" (Colossians 3:12). Jesus has taken the place that self used to have in their lives, so they don't find it impossible to forgive as Jesus forgave. His humility isn't a matter of constantly putting Himself down in His words or thoughts. He is tender*hearted*. His heart is full of compassion and kindness, meekness and patience—the sweet Spirit recognized as the heart of the Lamb of God.

Disciples want to grow, and they should. But their aim shouldn't be just for more boldness, joy, contempt for the world, zeal, or self-sacrifice. Even pagan philosophers who write self-help books and preach self-improvement would embrace those goals! *What set Jesus apart from all the good intentions on earth was the way He took up His cross daily.* Death to self—becoming poor in Spirit, meek, humble and lowly—was Jesus' aim. That heart is what He brought to earth from Heaven. And that heart is how we show our Christ-likeness. We must die to self in our dealings with the lost, for sure. But most of all we must pick up our cross in our dealings with God's people—denying ourselves for them, as Jesus did for us.

Fellow Christian, please take a good, hard look at what the Bible says a humble person is like. And please ask those walking with you whether they recognize in you a reproduction of the Original. Let's not settle for anything less than believing that each of the scriptures we have looked at is a promise of what God can and will do in our lives! Let's take those scriptures as a description in words of what the Spirit of Jesus will birth inside of us. Let's allow our failures and shortcomings drive us to the arms of the humble Lamb of God. Believe completely that where He is enthroned in the heart, His humility and gentleness will be one of the streams of living water that flow from within us.

Let me repeat: I feel deeply that we don't even realize how much the God's people are suffering because they haven't emptied themselves to make room for His power. When people try to serve Jesus together, all too often they find it impossible to be patient with one another, to love one another, to keep the unity of the Spirit through the bond of peace. People who should have experienced the deep joy of working as partners instead are a hindrance and burden to each other. All for one reason—the lack of the humility that considers self as nothing and rejoices in being the least, and only wants, like Jesus, to be the servant and helper of others, even of the least deserving.

Why do people who joyfully commit themselves to the cause of Christ find it so hard to commit themselves to their brothers and sisters? Isn't it because we have so little taught that the humility of Christ is the most important virtue and highest goal we can aim for by God's Spirit? But let's not be discouraged. Let the discovery that we lack humility motivate us to expect more from God than we've experienced. Let us look at every difficult, testing situation as an opportunity to grow. Let us look at difficult people as God's instrument for our purification. The Life of Jesus is breathing inside our hearts! And let's truly *believe* that God is everything and we are nothing, so that we may—by God's power—seek only to serve one another in love.

> *"I knew Jesus, and He was very precious to my soul; but I found something in me that would not keep sweet and patient and kind. I did what I could to keep it down, but it was there. I besought Jesus to do something for me, and when I gave Him my will, He came to my heart, and took out all that would not be sweet, all that would not be kind, all that would not be patient, and then He shut the door."*—George Foxe

7. Humility and Holiness

"...Yet they say to each other, 'Don't come too close or you will defile me! I am holier than you!' They are a stench in my nostrils..." (Isaiah 65:5).

We sometimes talk about "the Holiness Movement." We sing "I want to be holy, set apart for You, my Master, ready to do Your will." We hear about holiness teachings and meetings. The truths of holiness in Christ and holiness by faith can be found in countless books. But is the holiness we claim to have and seek alive and true in us? If you want to know the answer, ask yourself *whether it produces an increasing humility in us.* Humility is the one thing needed to allow God's holiness to live inside you and shine through you. Jesus, the Holy One of God, is the only One who can make us holy, too. Divine humility was the secret of His life, death, and resurrection. The only genuine proof of our holiness is humility before God and man. Humility is the bloom and beauty of holiness.

Counterfeit holiness can be recognized by its lack of genuine humility. Every one who seeks holiness should be on guard so that he or she doesn't carelessly stumble into this trap. "After starting your Christian lives in the Spirit," you can lapse into "trying to become perfect by your own human effort" (Galatians 3:3). Pride can creep in where it is least expected. Two men went into the temple to pray, one a Pharisee, the other a tax collector. The "Pharisee" can worm his way into any place, no matter how sacred, if we let him. Pride can rear its head in the very temple of God, and can degrade the worship of God into a showcase for self-life.

Sometimes the Pharisee can even disguise himself in the clothes of a tax collector! People who confess their deep sinfulness need to be just as careful as those who claim a deep holiness. Right when you want your heart to become the temple of God, you will probably find those two men coming in to pray. And the "tax collector" will find that the greatest danger is not from the Pharisee next to him, who despises him, but from the Pharisee inside him, who congratulates himself on how well he repents! In God's temple, when we think we are in the Most Holy Place, let's be on guard against pride. Remember, even the devil can enter God's presence. "One day the angels came to present themselves before the Lord, and satan the accuser came with them" (Job 1:6).

"I thank you, God, that I am not a sinner like everyone else, especially like that tax collector over there" (Luke 28:11). Instead of being truly thankful to God, self uses His blessing as an excuse to be complacent. In the very act of confessing that God has done it all, self finds a way to take credit. Yes, even in the temple, with the words of repentance and praise echoing off the walls, the Pharisee may chime right in, and in thanking God be congratulating himself. Pride can dress itself up in the clothing of religion.

We may laugh at someone who would be so blatant as to say, "I thank you that I am not like everybody else." But that same attitude can often be found in our own feelings or words towards others. Do you want proof? Walk into any religious assembly or Bible study or home group or "men's business meeting," and simply watch and listen for a while. How much of the "no beauty or majesty" of Jesus will you find? Will deep humility be the keynote of what the servants of Jesus are saying of themselves or each other? Are there not many congregations, conventions, "missions," committees, schools, and "ministries" where the harmony has been disturbed and God's work hindered? And isn't it usually all because people who are considered faithful Christians have proved—by touchiness and impatience, by self-defense and self-assertion, by sharp judgments and unkind words—that they do not consider others better than themselves? Is it not because the popular brand of "holiness" doesn't include humility as its main ingredient?

It is one thing to experience a season of great humbling and brokenness. It is another thing entirely to have a humble spirit, to be clothed in humility, to have the mind of Christ that considers self to be the servant of all.

"Don't come to close or you will defile me! I am holier than you!" That's not holiness—it's a bad joke. Jesus the Holy One is also the Humble One. The holiest will also be the humblest. There is no one holy but God. We have as much holiness as we have of Him. And what's really of God will show itself in genuine humility. Humility is simply the disappearance of self in the vision of God's holiness. We're too well mannered to boast openly like the Jews of Isaiah's day. But the same spirit is often seen in professing Christian's treatment of fellow believers or of the lost. In the attitude in which they offer opinions or try to work for God, their clothing can be tax collector but their hearts total Pharisee: "I thank you that I am not like everybody else."

Is there any remedy for this false humility? There is. "Love is patient and kind. Love is not jealous or boastful or proud or rude. Love does not demand its own way. Love is not irritable, and it keeps no record of when it has been wronged" (1 Corinthians 13:4-5). The power of *agape* love forgets itself and finds its blessedness in blessing others. It bears with them and honors them. The power of this love exists wherever the Spirit of Love has been poured into a human heart, wherever the divine nature has been birthed inside a person's life, and wherever Christ, the humble Lamb of God, is formed within. When God comes in, He brings *agape* love with Him, for God is love. When God has entered in power and given a revelation of Himself, a man or woman becomes nothing. And when a person becomes nothing before God, he or she cannot help but be humble before others. God's presence becomes more than something a person *feels* during a special song, but a constant covering under which the soul continually *lives*. Its deep humility before God becomes a holy root from which all words and works come forth.

May God teach us that our thoughts and words and feelings about other people are the true test of our humility toward Him! May He teach us that our humility before Him is the only power that can enable us to be always humble before others! Our humility must be the life of Christ, the Lamb of God, inside us.

Are you planning to teach others about holiness? Are you planning to seek it for yourself? Then be on your guard. There is no pride so dangerous or subtle as religious pride. No one will ever say, "Don't come too close or you will defile me." Most people would never even form those exact words in their minds. But there can grow in your heart subconsciously a secret habit of patting yourself on your back for your accomplishments. You can find yourself addicted to the drug of comparing yourself to others. You'll recognize this spiritual disease, not always by the presence of blatant words or actions, but by the presence of self dominating your thoughts. Those with discernment will detect it in your tone and countenance. Even the world won't be too impressed—in fact, you'll be giving them one more excuse to harden themselves to spiritual things. Only you will find yourself such a fascinating topic. When you've seen the glory of God for real, your attitude will be very, very different (Job 42:5-6; Isaiah 6:5).

Brothers and sisters, let's do take this warning seriously. Unless an increase in humility is truly our heart's desire, we may wake up one day to discover that we have been delighting in beautiful thoughts and feelings, in solemn words and actions, while the true evidence of God's presence—the disappearance of self—is nowhere to be found. Let's run to Jesus and hide ourselves in Him until we are clothed in His humility. There is no other way to find holiness.

8. Humility and Sin

"This is a true saying, and everyone should believe it:
Christ Jesus came into the world to save sinners—and
I was the worst of them all" (1 Timothy 1:15).

In our minds, we often link the word "humility" with certain bad feelings about ourselves that we are such terrible sinners. So we have a hard time imagining any other way to keep humble but to focus our thoughts on our sins. By now, I hope, we all realize that humility means much, much more. We have seen that Jesus' teachings and the apostolic writings strongly emphasize humility, often without mentioning sin at all. Long before sin entered into the picture, God created the universe to run on submission and surrender. Jesus Himself lived a life of perfect humility, and He never sinned. And the humility He imparts to us is not to make us think about sin *more*, but to practice sin much *less*. Humility has less to do with sin than with holiness and blessing. It is about *self* moving out of the way so that *God* can take the throne. When God is everything, self is nothing.

That aspect of the truth is what I've mostly wanted to stress. But having said all of that, I do want to emphasize that God's grace in the face of our sin really should create a new depth and intensity to humility for every child of His. We only need to look at a man like Paul to see how, throughout his life as a blood-bought man of God, he never forgot the sinner he had been.

We all know the passages where Paul refers to his life as a persecutor and blasphemer. "For I am the least of all the apostles, and I am not worthy to be called an apostle after the way I persecuted the church of God" (1 Corinthians 15:9-10). "Just think! Though I did nothing to deserve it, and though I am the least deserving Christian there is, I was chosen for this special joy of telling the Gentiles about the endless treasures available to them in Christ" (Ephesians 3:9). "How thankful I am to Christ Jesus our Lord for considering me trustworthy and appointing me to serve Him, even though I used to scoff at the name of Christ. I hunted down His people, harming them in every way I could. But God had mercy on me because I did it in ignorance and unbelief" (1 Timothy 1:12-13).

God's grace had saved Paul. He remembered Paul's sin no more. But never, never could Paul forget how terribly he had sinned. The more he rejoiced in God's salvation and the more his experience of God's grace filled him with an unspeakable joy, the clearer his awareness became that he was a saved sinner. He realized that salvation would have no meaning or sweetness unless the sense of his being a sinner made it precious and real to him. Not for a single moment could Paul forget that it was a sinner whom God had taken up in His arms and crowned with His love.

The passages we quoted weren't a confession of sin that Paul was still practicing daily—just read them carefully in their context and that much should be obvious. But they have a far deeper meaning. They refer to something that will last forever, not just for a day. This awareness of our sin will give a deep, rich awe and wonder to our humility when we bow before the throne. They will take the position of those who have been washed from their sins by the blood of the Lamb. Never, never—even in glory— can they be anything but ransomed sinners. Not for a moment in this life can God's children live in the full light of His love without understanding that the sin they were saved from is their only qualification for all that God's grace has promised to do in them.

It takes humility for us to come to Christ as sinners. That humility takes on new meaning when we realize how fitting it is for us as new creations. Yet even then, the humility birthed in us has its deepest, richest notes of praise when we remember what it is to be a monument of God's wondrous, redeeming love.

The full impact of Paul's teachings about humility hits us when we realize how nearly sinless a life he lived after his rebirth. In the book of Acts and in the letters, we read of great disciples who fell into one sin or another. Even Peter sinned. But what sin could we charge Paul with? It's not that he wasn't vulnerable, either. In his letters he laid bare his heart in intensely personal ways. But where can we detect any shortcoming or defect? Where can we say he failed in his duty, or sinned against the perfect law of love?

Paul could write some amazing statements in his letters. "You yourselves are our witnesses—and so is God—that we are pure and honest and faultless toward all of you believers" (1 Thessalonians 2:10). "We can say with confidence and a clear conscience that we have been honest and sincere in all our dealings" (2 Corinthians 1:12). Paul wasn't speaking of how he *aspired* to live. He was saying quite matter-of-factly that these statements described how he *had* lived. Whatever else we may say about these passages, we have to admit Paul must have lived in the Power of the Holy Spirit to a degree that has seldom if ever been matched.

My point is this: the secret to Paul's humility simply couldn't have been that he was obsessed with thinking about his daily sin. Instead, his secret can be found in how he *positioned* himself continually in his heart, a position he never forgot for a moment. And the more God's provision abounded to him, the more alive that position became in him. That position is our only true place—the only place of blessing. *We must take the place of those whose highest joy is to confess that they are sinners saved by grace.*

Paul remembered vividly his terrible sins in the past, before he knew God's grace. He knew just as vividly that only God's transforming power kept him from sinning now. And he never forgot that the dark, hidden monster of self was always lurking nearby, ready to burst back in, but held back by the presence and power of Jesus living in his heart. "I know that I am rotten through and through as far as my old sinful nature is concerned" (Romans 7:18). These words will describe the flesh to the end of our lives. "For the power of the life-giving Spirit has freed you through Christ Jesus from the power of sin that leads to death" (Romans 8:2). This glorious freedom doesn't mean that the flesh is annihilated. It also doesn't mean that the flesh is somehow rehabilitated. Instead, it means that the Spirit continuously gives us victory as He puts to death the misdeeds of the flesh.

A healthy body kills germs. Light swallows up darkness. Life conquers death. And Jesus, living in you through His Spirit, is the health and light and life of your soul. But with this conviction comes another, that our helplessness is only overcome as we trust the continual working of the Holy Spirit. We have a humble sense of our dependence on Him. Faith and joy are the companions of humility. This humility lives only by the grace of God.

The three scriptures we quoted above all show that it was the wonderful grace given Paul—a grace he knew he needed every moment—that humbled him so deeply. God's provision enabled him to work harder than the rest. It is the nature of grace that it enables the saved sinner to declare to unbelievers the unsearchable riches of Christ. With this extravagant grace come faith in and love for the Lord Jesus. It was this grace that kept Paul's consciousness of having once sinned, and being still capable of sin, so intensely alive. "As people sinned more and more, God's wonderful kindness became more abundant" (Romans 5:20). Grace demolishes sin. The greater our experience of grace, the more intense will be our awareness that we are sinners. It isn't *sin* that keeps us truly humble, but God's *grace*. Sin doesn't make me realize I am a sinner; grace does. Grace makes the sinner's position of deep humility a place I will never leave.

I'm afraid that there are many people who have tried to humble themselves by condemning themselves strongly and putting themselves down, but who still would have to admit that a humble spirit, together with kindness, compassion, meekness, and forbearance, are as far off as ever. Focusing on yourself—even with self-hatred—will never free you from yourself. You need God's revelation, not only through His law condemning you, but also through his grace delivering you. Then you will be humble.

The law may break your heart with fear. But only grace can work into your heart the sweet humility that becomes its nature and its joy. It was the revelation of God in His holiness, drawing near to make Himself known in His grace, that made Abraham and Jacob, Job and Isaiah, bow so low before Him. There will be no room for self in the soul that waits for, trusts, worships, and is filled with the presence of God the Creator as everything for man in his nothingness, and God the Redeemer as everything for man in his sinfulness. In only this way can the promise be fulfilled: "The arrogance of all people will be brought low. Their pride will lie in the dust. The Lord alone will be exalted!" (Isaiah 2:17)

It is the sinner, stepping into the full light of God's holy, redeeming love, who will experience God's love living inside him through Christ and the Holy Spirit. That person cannot help but be humble. Not to focus on sin, but to focus on Jesus, will bring you deliverance from self.

9. Humility and Faith

"No wonder you can't believe! For you gladly honor each other, but you don't care about the honor that comes from God alone" (John 5:44).

Recently I heard someone say that the blessings of discipleship are like the goods displayed in a shop window—you can see them clearly, but you can't touch them. If someone told a window shopper to reach out and pick up one of the items for sale, he or she would answer, "I can't. There is a thick pane of glass between me and that thing." In the same way, Christians can admire God's awesome promises. "You will experience God's peace, which is far more wonderful than the human mind can understand. His peace will guard your hearts and minds as you live in Christ Jesus" (Philippians 4:7). "Come to me, all of you who are weary and carry heavy burdens, and I will give you rest" (Matthew 11:28). "He has given us the Holy Spirit to fill our hearts with His love" (Romans 5:5). "Even now you are happy with a glorious, inexpressible joy" (1 Peter 1:8). Yet very many people feel that there is an invisible something standing between them and those promises, so that they can see them but not truly possess them. And what is that barrier? *Pride.*

The promises made to the believing heart are so free and certain, the invitation and encouragement to receive those promises are so strong, and God's mighty power to make good on those promises is so available. Only something capable of hindering our hearts from believing could stand in the way of those promises becoming real to us. Jesus tells us what that hindrance is: "No wonder you can't believe! For you gladly honor each other, but you don't care about the honor that comes from God alone." Faith and pride are enemies. Faith and humility are allies. We can never have more of genuine faith than we have of genuine humility. True, we can still have strong convictions in our *minds* while there is pride in our *hearts*, but a living faith, bursting with the power of God, is impossible.

What is faith, anyway? Doesn't it mean confessing that we are nothing and helpless on our own, and surrendering to God and allowing Him to work? What could be more humbling than to accept that we are dependent on Someone else, and that we have no rights to claim or receive anything except what He's gracious enough to give us? Humility is simply the attitude of heart that prepares you to live by trusting God. Clinging to a scrap of pride, even in secret—by selfishness or stubbornness or arrogance or grabbing after attention—strengthens your flesh. And remember, flesh cannot inherit the Kingdom or receive Kingdom blessings. Self-life refuses to allow God to be what He is and must always be—your Everything!

Faith is a spiritual organ. As the eyes enable you to perceive the physical world, faith allows you to see the unseen. Through faith you see "Him who is invisible." With faith, you aren't limited to walking by sight. Pride seeks—and jealously guards—the attention and praise and reputation available in the seen realm to those who chase after it. Faith, on the other hand, rejects selfish ambition and contents itself with whatever honor God offers from His throne. As long as we're chasing after the seen realm's blessings, we can't be seeking blessing in the unseen realm. *Pride makes faith impossible.* Salvation comes through a cross and a crucified Christ. Salvation means having fellowship with a crucified Christ in the Spirit of His cross. Salvation is union with, delight in, and participation in the humility of Jesus. No wonder our faith is so feeble if pride still controls us so much! Are we willing to long and pray for humility as the most critical and blessed part of salvation?

Humility and faith are joined in the Scriptures more than many people realize. Twice Jesus praised someone for having great faith. The centurion said, "I am not worthy for You to come into my home." He then acknowledged Jesus' authority. Jesus was amazed and replied, "I haven't seen faith like this in all the land of Israel!" (Matthew 8:8,20) The gentile woman threw herself at Jesus' feet and said, "Yes, Lord, but even dogs are permitted to eat the crumbs that fall beneath their master's table." Jesus answered, "Woman, your faith is great" (Matthew 15:27-28). The humility that brings a man or a woman to the point of being nothing before God at the same time removes every obstacle to faith. Humility makes the soul fear that it would dishonor Him by not trusting Him completely.

Brothers and sisters, haven't we discovered here the real reason for our failures in pursuing holiness? Isn't it pride that has made our consecration and faith so superficial and short-lived? We had no idea how much pride and self were still secretly working in us. We were not aware of how God alone, by coming in with His mighty power, could cast them out. We did not understand how only a new heart, created to be like God, could really make us humble. We did not know that total, constant, complete humility must be the foundation for every prayer and approach to God and for all our dealings with people. We did not realize that we might as well try to see without eyes or breathe without lungs as to believe and draw near to God without humility and lowliness of heart.

It makes no sense to strive and strive to have faith, when all the time our prideful old self-life is working behind the scenes, trying to manipulate God to gain blessings. No wonder some people just can't seem to believe. What we need is a total change of direction. First, let's seek to humble ourselves under the mighty hand of God. He will lift us up. The cross, the death, and the tomb where Jesus humbled Himself were His path to the glory of God. Our path lies there, too. Let our one desire and fervent prayer be to humble ourselves like Jesus. Let us gladly accept whatever can humble us before God or others—this alone is the path to His glory.

Maybe you are wondering about people who seem blessed and who even seem able to bless others, but who have little apparent humility. Does that prove that God has honored their faith, even though they clearly are seeking the honor that comes from men? If such people do have even a measure of faith, and if

God has bestowed on them special spiritual gifts, then to the measure they do believe they will be able to bless others. But even in that blessing, their faith—and therefore their impact—are stunted by their pride. The blessing that could have resulted in eternal fruit is actually superficial or temporary, just because they refuse to become nothing to open the way for God to be All. A deeper humility would have brought a deeper and fuller blessing. If these men had allowed God's Holy Spirit to live in them in the fullness of His grace—not just to gift them with some special ability—He would have produced in them a life of power, holiness, and perseverance that is all too rare in our day.

"No wonder you can't believe! For you gladly honor each other, but you don't care about the honor that comes from God alone." Only one thing can cure you from the desire to receive honor from others. Only one thing can free you from the hypersensitivity and pain and anger that enslave you when you don't get that honor. Give yourself to seek only the honor that comes from God. Let the glory of the all-glorious God be everything to you. You will be delivered from slavery to self, and you will be content and glad to get nothing for yourself out of what you do. Out of this nothingness you will grow strong in faith, giving glory to God. You will make a wonderful discovery: the deeper you sink in humility before Him, the nearer He is to fulfill every desire of your faith.

10. Humility and Death to Self

"In human form He obediently humbled Himself even further by dying a criminal's death on the cross" (Philippians 2:8).

Humility will take you down a path leading to death. Death to self is humility's destination. When Jesus humbled Himself to the point of death, He blazed a new trail for us to walk in. There was only one way for Jesus to prove His utter surrender to His Father. There was only one way for Him to rise beyond His humanness and return to His Father—the cross. The cross is our only way, too.

Humility must lead us to die to self. We have no other way to become real. It is the only way we can die to our fallen nature and alive to God. Only through our own cross can we have Christ formed in us. Humility will be the air He breathes inside us. Humility will be His joy.

Jesus gave His disciples Resurrection Life. The glorified and enthroned Lamb actually came down from heaven to live inside them through His Spirit. Jesus won the power to accomplish these things by His death. The Life He gives is a life born out of death. Jesus' Life was surrendered to death and won back from death. The One who came to live inside of them was the One who could say: "I am the Living One who died. Look, I am alive forever and ever! And I hold the keys of death and the grave" (Revelation 1:18). His Life and Person and Presence bear the marks of being born out of death.

In His disciples, that life bears the death-marks, too. When the Spirit of the Crucified One lives and works in the heart, the power of His Life can be known. The most important mark of Jesus' death is humility. Only humility leads to the cross, and only the cross can perfect humility. Humility and death to self are two ways of describing the same thing. Humility is the bud; in death to self, the fruit is ripened to perfection.

Humility will cause you to die to self. Humility means giving up self and coming to a place of complete nothingness before God. Jesus humbled Himself and became obedient to the point of death. On the cross He gave the most convincing proof possible that He had abandoned His will to the God's will. In dying, He let go of Himself, with all of His natural reluctance to "drink the cup." He gave up the life He had taken on when He became a man. He died to self and to all temptations to sin. For the first time, a Man entered into the perfect Life of God. If it had not been for His infinite humility, considering Himself merely a servant to do God's will and to suffer for it, He would never have embraced the cross.

How can you and I die to ourselves? What does that phrase even mean, practically? Look to Jesus for the answer. Death to self is not your work; it is God's work. In Christ you are dead to sin. The Life inside you, if you belong to Him, has gone through death and resurrection. You can be certain you are in truth dead to sin. But if you want the power of this "union with Christ in His death" to explode in your character and conduct, you must allow the Holy Spirit to work it into you. You need Him to teach you. If you really want to enter into full fellowship with Jesus in His death and experience total deliverance from self, then *humble yourself.* Voluntary humility is your one responsibility.

Fall on your face before God in your utter helplessness. Face the facts squarely: you are unable to put your old life to death, and you are unable to make yourself live again. Sink down into your own nothingness. Take the attitude of meek, patient, and trusting surrender to God. Embrace what humbles you. Look on every frustration as a tool to humble you. Take full advantage of every opportunity to humble yourself before others so you can stay humble before God. God can reveal Christ in you only through the mighty strengthening of His Spirit. Christ will be truly formed in you in His form as a servant. He will fill your heart. God will honor each deliberate choice you make to humble yourself, accepting it as a sacrifice, and using it to clear the way for His Son to reveal Himself in you. The path of humility leads to the death of self-life, and the full and perfect experience of the wonderful truth that you are dead in Christ.

This death to self will, in turn, lead to complete humility. Some have wanted to be humble, but were afraid to be too humble. Don't make that mistake! Don't place stipulations and limitations on your humility. Don't add fine print to the covenant you make with God! Don't try to figure it all out—abandon your heart first, then you'll know how to live it out. Humble yourself to the point of death. It is in death to self that humility reaches completion. Know for certain that at the root of all genuine experience of growth in grace and consecration and transformation, there must be a death to self—something real, that demonstrates itself to God and men in our character and habits.

It is sadly possible for us to talk on and on about the crucified life and the Spirit-walk, when those who love us best would still have to admit that they see much self-life in us. Physical life is pronounced dead when the heart stops beating and the brain waves stop functioning. Self-life is pronounced dead when there is a humility present that doesn't cling to reputation, that empties itself and takes the form of a servant. It is possible to speak much and speak sincerely of fellowship with a despised and rejected Jesus, and of bearing His cross, while the meek, lowly, kind, and gentle humility of the Lamb of God is not seen—or even truly sought. The title "Lamb of God" means humility and death. Let us receive the Lamb in both forms. You can't separate them in Jesus; they should be joined in us, too.

If dying to self depended on us, how hopeless we would be! Flesh can't overcome flesh, even with grace's help. Self can never cast out self, even in someone who is born again. Praise God! The work has been finished forever. The death of Jesus, who offered Himself once for all, is our death to self. And the ascension of Jesus, who once and for all sat down at the right hand of God, has made it possible for Him to pour His Spirit into our hearts.

"His divine power gives us everything we need for living a godly life. He has called us to receive His own glory and goodness! And by that same mighty power, He has given us all of His rich and wonderful promises. He has promised that you will escape the decadence all around you caused by evil desires and that you will share in His divine nature" (2 Peter 1:3-4).

As the disciple follows in the steps of Jesus in the pursuit and practice of humility, his or her hunger for something more is awakened. A desire and hope spring to life. Faith begins growing stronger. It learns to look up and claim and receive true fullness in the Spirit of Jesus. That fullness has the power to put sin and self to death daily. For true disciples, humility is the fragrance and nature of their lives together.

"Have you forgotten that when we became Christians and were baptized to become one with Christ Jesus, we died with Him?... So you should consider yourselves dead to sin and able to live for the glory of God through Christ Jesus...Give yourselves completely to God since you have been given a new life. And use your whole body as a tool to do what is right for the glory of God" (Romans 6:3,11, 13). The whole thought process of a disciple is to be saturated by the Spirit that led Jesus to the cross. Disciples present themselves to God as those who have died in Christ and in Him risen from the dead, bearing in their hearts the nail prints of His cross. Both death to self and resurrection power are visible their genuine, practical, moment-by-moment humility before God and men.

Believer, claim in faith the death and the life of Jesus as yours. Enter into His rest. Jesus committed His Spirit into the Father's hands. So must you as you humble yourself and descend each day into total, helpless dependence on God. He will raise you up and honor you. Each morning, sink into the tomb of Jesus by making a concrete choice before Him that your life will not be your own this day. As you live the rest of the day, keep reaffirming that choice, and the Life of Jesus will be seen in you. Let a willing, loving, peaceful, and happy humility be the evidence that you have indeed claimed your birthright—baptism into the death of Christ. "By that one offering He has perfected forever those who are being made holy" (Hebrews 10:14). The hearts that enter into His humility will find in Him the power to consider self as dead and—as those who have received and learned of Him—to live in yieldedness and servanthood, supporting one another in love. Death to self is seen in a humility like Jesus had.

11. Humility and Happiness

"Each time he said, 'My gracious favor is all you need. My power works best in your weakness.' So now I am glad to boast about my weaknesses, so that the power of Christ may work through me. Since I know it is all for Christ's good, I am quite content with my weaknesses and with insults, hardships, persecutions, and calamities. For when I am weak, then I am strong" (2 Corinthians 12:9-10).

God had given Paul an awesome revelation. To keep him from becoming proud, God also gave him "a thorn in the flesh." Paul's first reaction was to ask God to remove the thorn—in fact, that was his second and third reaction, too! But Jesus answered that the trial was really a blessing, that in the weakness it brought, His grace and strength could become more real. So Paul immediately took a new attitude towards his thorn. Instead of simply *enduring* it, he became "glad to boast about it." Instead of asking for deliverance, he rejoiced in it. Paul had learned that the place of humility is the place of blessing, power, and joy.

Most Christians who pursue humility go through those same two stages. At first, they fear and recoil and ask for deliverance from the humbling situation. They have to learn to seek humility at any cost. They have accepted the command to be humble and are trying to obey it, but they keep finding themselves failing miserably. They pray for humility, sometimes very intensely. But in their secret hearts they pray even harder—in thought, if not in actual words—to be protected from the very things that will make them humble. They aren't yet to the point where they love humility as the beauty of the Lamb of God and the joy of heaven, and so they aren't ready to sell everything to have it. In their pursuit of humility and prayer for it, there is a feeling that somehow humility is still a burden and a bondage, after all. Humbling themselves hasn't yet become the spontaneous expression of a life and character that is humble from the inside out. Humility is not yet their pleasure and joy. They can't say, "I am glad to boast about my weaknesses; I am grateful for everything that humbles me."

Can we ever hope to reach that point? Definitely! What will get us there? The same thing that brought Paul there—*a new revelation of the Lord Jesus.* When more of Jesus can move in, more of self will move out. Paul got a much clearer insight into the deep truth that the presence of Jesus will banish our every desire to seek anything for ourselves. The more we see of Jesus, the more we will be willing to embrace whatever humbles us, to make an even larger place for Him in our hearts. Our trials will teach us, as we experience the power and presence of Jesus, to choose humility as our highest blessing. Let's learn from Paul's example.

There are many people who are looked to for leadership, who have experienced God's blessings, who have become teachers of others, who have yet to learn humility. Paul knew this danger. He realized the potential he had to become puffed up with self-importance. Yet he needed to learn more fully what it meant to become nothing—to die that Christ might live in him. It was still hard for him to be glad for his trials. The next stage in his growth was to learn to be more like Jesus in emptying himself, to boast in his weaknesses so that Jesus could be strong.

The highest lesson a believer has to learn is humility. Do you want to grow in holiness? Then remember: the road to holiness passes through humbling experiences. You could have intense consecration, fervent zeal, and deep experiences, but unless you receive God's special dealings to humble you, you could grow prideful and self-important. Let's never forget that the highest holiness is the deepest humility. And humility only comes if we give God permission to lead us through whatever discipline He requires to train us. He is our Faithful Lord.

Let's look at our lives in light of Paul's experience and see if we, too, gladly boast in our weaknesses, if we consider it pure joy when we experience trial, need, and trouble. Have we learned to regard a criticism, whether fair or not, as an opportunity to draw near to Jesus in quietness and peace? What about when someone brings us into a situation of trouble or difficulty that we didn't ask for? Will we accept that our own pleasure and honor are worthless? Will we be grateful for the humbling? It is a great blessing—the deep happiness of heaven—to be so free from self that whatever is said about us or done to us is lost and swallowed up in the thought that Jesus is our inheritance.

Let's trust the same Jesus who took charge of Paul to take charge of us, too. Paul needed special discipline and teaching to learn something even more precious than the "things so astounding they can't be told" that he had heard in the third heaven. He needed to learn how to boast in weakness! We need that lesson too—oh, so much. Jesus, who cared for Paul, will care for us, too. He watches over us with a jealous, loving care, to keep *us* from getting puffed up by *our* revelations of Him. If we start becoming proud or pompous, He shows us our evil and brings us experiences to deliver us from it. In trial and weakness and trouble, He seeks to bring us low, until we learn that His grace is enough for us and take pleasure in what makes and keeps us humble. His power working through weakness, His presence filling and satisfying our emptiness, becomes the secret of a humility that will never fail. In view of God's mercies, we can learn to say with Paul, "I am not at all inferior to these 'super apostles,' even *though I am nothing at all*" (2 Corinthians 12:11). Paul's trials had led him to true humility. With humility, he had received a wonderful joy and pleasure and "boasting" about his difficulties.

"Since I know it is all for Christ's good, I am quite content with my weaknesses and with insults, hardships, persecutions, and calamities." The humble man has learned the secret of contentment. The more pressed he feels, the more difficult life becomes, the more he experiences the presence and power of Jesus. As he admits he is nothing, the Word of God comes with deepening joy: "My gracious favor is all you need" (2 Corinthians 12:9).

To sum it up: the danger of pride is greater and nearer than we realize—and the grace for humility is, too.

The danger of pride is greater and nearer than we realize, especially at the time of our richest blessings. When God's provision is present with powerful effect, when miracles are happening, when others take notice, there are hidden, subconscious dangers there. Paul was in danger without knowing it. What Jesus did for him is recorded for our learning so that we could recognize our own dangers and realize our only Place of safety. Let's not give a single person the excuse to say that someone who proclaims Jesus is full of self and that Christians don't practice what they preach. Jesus, in whom we trust, can make us humble.

But yes, the grace for humility is greater than we think, too. The humility of Jesus is our salvation. Jesus Himself is our humility. Our humility is His concern and His work. His grace is more than enough for us to meet the temptation of pride, too. His strength will work best in our weakness. Let's choose to admit our weakness, to be low, to be nothing. Let humility become our joy.

Let us be glad to boast about our own weaknesses, about everything that can humble us and keep us low. The power of Christ will rest upon us. Christ humbled Himself, and so God honored Him. Christ will humble us, and keep us humble. Let's join our hearts fully to His work! Let's trustingly and joyfully accept everything that humbles us. We will discover that the deepest humility is the secret of the truest happiness, of a joy that no one can take away.

12. Humility and Exaltation

"For the proud will be humbled, but the humble will be honored" (Luke 14:11; 18:14).

"When you bow down before the Lord and admit your dependence on Him, He will lift you up and give you honor" (James 4:10).

"So humble yourselves under the mighty power of God, and in His good time He will honor you" (1 Peter 5:6).

Just yesterday someone asked me, "How can I conquer this pride?" The answer is simple. Two things are needed. Do what God says is your work—humble yourself. Trust God for what He says is *His* work—He will lift you up.

The command is clear: humble yourself. That doesn't mean you have the ability to conquer and cast out the pride of your heart and to form within yourself the lowliness of the Holy Jesus. No, that's God's work. When He says He will "honor you" and "lift you up," He means that He will form that character of Jesus in you. Your part in the process is to take every opportunity of humbling yourself before God and man. Stand firm. Don't let any failure convince you to quit. His command will never change. Persevere with faith in the grace that is already working in you and with full confidence in the grace God will give for the victory that's coming. Look to the light God provides, through your conscience within you and your brothers and sisters around you, to expose the pride of your heart and its workings.

Accept with gratitude everything that God allows from inside or outside, from friend or enemy, by seemingly natural means or by miraculous ones, to remind you of your need of humbling, and to help you to it. Believe that humility to indeed the mother of all godly character, your most important duty to God, and the best safeguard for your heart. Set your heart on it, because it is the source of blessing. God's promise is sure: "the humble will be honored." See that you do the one thing God asks, and humble yourself. God will see that He does the one thing He promised. He will give you more grace. When the time is right, He will honor you and lift you up.

God's dealings with us usually come in two stages. First there is a time of preparation. God's commands and His promises join forces to train and disciple us for something higher. We will experience effort and inability, partial success followed by seeming failure, mingled with a holy hunger for more of Jesus. Then comes the time of fulfillment, when faith inherits the promise and enjoys what it had so often struggled for in vain. All true disciples will experience these two stages often. Somehow, God created the universe so that we'd grow in that way.

In His efforts to redeem us, God always makes the first move. Then man's turn comes. He struggles to obey and live up to his calling, but he comes to realize his desperate weakness. In self-despair, he must learn to die to himself, with his willing cooperation and full consent. In the end, man longs for God, not victory. That's when faith is ready to receive God's promise. The Father will finish the work that man didn't even understand at the start. God began the process, and He will end it, even if man doesn't understand Him or His purposes at first.

That dynamic describes our pursuit of humility, too. To every Christian the command comes from the throne of God: humble yourself. When we respond with a serious attempt to listen and obey, God will reward—yes, reward—us with a painful discovery. We will find we have a shocking amount of pride— an unwillingness to consider ourselves nothing and to let others to consider us nothing, too. We will also discover an utter weakness to all our efforts, even in our prayers to God for help, to destroy the hideous monster of pride. Blessed is the person who now learns to put his or her hope in God and perseveres, despite all of the failures, in acts of humility before God and men.

Sow an act, reap a habit; sow a habit, reap a character; sow a character, reap a destiny. Grace works that way. God also has us repeat the act of humbling ourselves to produce a habit in us. "For God is working in you, giving you the desire to obey Him and the power to do what pleases Him" (Philippians 2:13). Come to God, humbling your proud heart before Him, and He will reward you with more grace, and replace your pride with humility. The Spirit of Jesus will conquer and bring a new nature to maturity inside you. He, the meek and lowly One, will live inside you forever.

"When you bow down before the Lord and admit your dependence on Him, He will lift you up and give you honor" (James 4:10). What is this honor? The highest honor for any man or woman is to be a vessel, to receive and enjoy and demonstrate God's glory. We can be that vessel only if we are willing to be nothing in ourselves so that God can be Everything for us. Water always fills the lowest places first. The lower and emptier a man bows before God, the quicker and fuller the inflow of God's glory will be.

The honor God promises isn't some external thing. All that He has to give is more of Himself. What does an earthly trophy really mean, anyway? It's just hardware. It doesn't really have anything to do with the achievement it's supposed to reward. But God's rewards are always genuine, meaningful, and the fruit of what we've sown. Sow a willingness to humble yourself, reap a divine humility inside you. That is God's highest honor— to be like His Son.

"So humble yourselves under the mighty power of God, and in His good time He will honor you." Jesus Himself is all the proof we need that these words are true. He is the guarantee that God will make good on this promise. Let us take His yoke on us and learn from Him, for He is humble and gentle. If we are just willing to lower ourselves for His sake, the way He lowered Himself for ours, He will bend down again, and we will find ourselves equally yoked with Him. As we enter deeper into the fellowship of His humility, we can count on Him. Whether we are humbling ourselves before others or being humbled by them, the Spirit of His honor, "the Spirit of our Glorious God," will rest on us. The presence and power of the glorified Christ will come to anyone who has a humble spirit.

When God can take His rightful place inside us, He will lift us up. Make His glory priority number one as you humble yourself. He will make your glory *His* priority as He perfects your humility. He will breathe into you, as your abiding life, the Spirit of His Son. As the Life of God saturates and possesses you, there will be nothing so natural and sweet as to *be* nothing. You won't need to think about self at all, because all of your attention will be focused on the One who is filling you. "So now I am glad to boast about my weaknesses, so that the power of Christ may work through me" (2 Corinthians 12:9).

Brothers and sisters, what is the real reason that our consecration and faith have made so little progress in the pursuit of holiness? Because self and its strength have been trying to work in the name of faith. We called God in to serve self and its happiness. Without realizing it, we were still trying to find life in improving ourselves. We never understood that humility—total, lasting, Christ-like humility, filling all of our life with God and man—was the most essential ingredient of the life of holiness we were seeking.

It is only in finding God that I lose myself. Have you ever looked in a sunbeam, with all its beauty and brightness, and seen a tiny speck of dust floating and dancing in it? That's what humility is like. Self becomes a little speck, bathed in the sunlight of His love.

> "How great is God! How small am I!
> Lost, swallowed up in Love's immensity!
> God only there, not I."

May God teach us to believe that to be humble, to be nothing in His presence, is the highest achievement and greatest blessing of the Christian life. "The high and lofty One who inhabits eternity, the Holy One, says this: 'I live in that high and holy place with those whose spirits are contrite and humble. I refresh the humble and give new courage to those with repentant hearts'" (Isaiah 57:15). May this destiny be ours!

> "Oh, to be emptier, lowlier,
> Mean, unnoticed, and unknown,
> And to God a vessel holier,
> Filled with Christ, and Christ alone!"

The Blood
of the Lamb
the Conquering
Weapon

They overcame him by the blood of the Lamb and by the word of their testimony; they did not love their lives so much as to shrink from death (Revelation 12:11).

The Conquering Weapon

Wherever evil appears, it is to be fought by the children of God in the name of Jesus and the power of the Holy Spirit. When evil appeared in an angel, at once there was war in heaven. Evil in mortal men is to be opposed by all regenerate men. If sin comes to us in the form of an angel of light, we must still war with it. If it comes with all kinds of unrighteous deception, we must not negotiate with it for a single moment, but begin the battle immediately, if we really belong to the armies of the Lord. Evil is at its very worst in satan himself: with him we fight. He is no ordinary adversary. Any one of the evil spirits under his control is a terrible foe. But when satan himself personally attacks a Christian, we will have the fight of our lives on our hands.

When this dragon blocks our road, we will need help from heaven to force our way through. A pitched battle with Apollyon may not occur often, but when it does, you will know it painfully. You will record it in your diary as one of the darkest days you have ever lived, and you will eternally praise your God, when you have overcome the enemy. But even if satan were ten times stronger and craftier than he is, it would be our duty to wrestle against him. We cannot for a moment hesitate or offer him a truce. Evil in its strongest and proudest form is to be attacked by the soldier of the cross, and nothing must end the war but complete victory. Satan is the enemy, the enemy of enemies. That prayer of our Lord's, which we usually render, "Deliver us from evil," has the special significance of "Deliver us from the evil one." He is the chief embodiment of evil, and in him evil is intensified and has come to its highest strength. Anyone who hopes to overcome this enemy of God and man needs to have Omnipotence on his side. Satan would destroy all godly ones if he could. Even though he cannot, he has such an incurable hatred that he is maliciously eager to harass those whom he cannot devour.

In Revelation 12 the devil is called an "enormous red dragon." He is enormous in ability, intelligence, energy, and experience. Whether he was the chief of all angels before he fell, I do not know. Some believe that he was, and that when he heard that a Man was going to sit on God's throne, out of jealousy he rebelled against the Most High. This is conjecture. But we do know that he was and is an enormously powerful spirit compared with us. He is a being great in evil—the prince of darkness, having the power of death. He shows his malice against the saints by accusing them day and night before God. In the prophets we can read of satan standing to accuse Joshua the High Priest. Satan also accused Job of serving God from selfish motives: "Have you not put a hedge around him and his household and everything he has?"

This ever active enemy desires to tempt as well as accuse: he demands to have us and sift us as wheat. In calling him the dragon, the Holy Spirit seems to hint at his mysterious power and character. To our limited understanding, a spirit such as satan must forever remain a mystery both in his person and his works. Although he is a mysterious being, he is absolutely not a mythical one. We can never doubt his existence once we have come into conflict with him. The fact that he is so mysterious only makes him more real. If he were flesh and blood, it would be far easier to contend with him. But to fight against "the spiritual forces of evil in the heavenly realms" is a frightening assignment. Like a dragon he is full of cunning and ferocity. In him power is joined with craftiness. If he cannot achieve his purpose quickly with brute force, he is willing to wait patiently. He deludes, and he deceives; in fact, he is said to deceive the whole world. What a power of deception must live inside him, since under his influence one third of the stars of heaven are flung to earth (Revelation 12:4), and millions of men in every age have worshipped demons and idols!

He has saturated the minds of men with deception, so that they cannot see that they should worship no one but God, their Maker. The devil is described as "that ancient serpent," reminding us how experienced he is in every evil skill. He was a liar from the beginning, and the father of lies. After thousands of years of constant practice in deception, he is much too cunning for us. If we think that we can match his craftiness, we are serious fools. He knows vastly more than the wisest of mortal humans. If we challenge him to a game of strategy, he will wipe us off the board, and sweep our pieces into the bag. He is not only shrewd, he is lightning fast. He is ready to attack at any moment, darting down upon us like a hawk upon its helpless prey. He cannot be everywhere at once, but it is hard to find a place at any given moment where he isn't. By his incredible power, he oversees his army of fallen demons like a great general. He directs the attack over the whole field of battle and seems present at every point. No door can shut him out. No height of goodness can rise beyond his reach. He meets us in all our weaknesses and attacks us from every point of the compass. He comes upon us unaware and injures us with wounds that are not easily healed.

But yet, dear friends, as powerful as this infernal spirit certainly is, his power is defeated when we resolve never to make peace with him. We must never dream of negotiating a truce with evil. To suppose that we can ignore him and everything will be fine is a deadly mistake. We must fight or die. Evil will kill us if we do not put it to death first. We can only find safety in a single-minded, energetic opposition to sin, whatever shape it takes, whatever it threatens, whatever it promises. The Holy Spirit alone can maintain in us this hatred of sin.

According to Revelation 12, the saints "overcame him." We must never rest until it can be said of us also, "They overcame him."

He is an enemy who deserves your opposition. Do you refuse the conflict? Do you think of turning back? You have no armor for your back. To quit fighting is to admit defeat. You have your choice. Either settle it in your mind that you are in for a life-long resistance, or else become satan's slave forever. I ask God that you wake up, get out of bed, and give battle to the adversary. Resolve once and for all that by the grace of God you will be numbered with those who overcome the archenemy.

The scriptures raise two very important points for us to consider: What is the conquering weapon? What sword did they use against the great red dragon when they overcame him? Listen! "They overcame him by the blood of the Lamb." *How do we use that weapon?* We must do as they did and overcome "by the word of our testimony" as we refuse to "love our lives so much as to shrink from death."

"They Overcame Him by the Blood of the Lamb"

The blood of the Lamb means the death of the Son of God. The sufferings of Jesus might be described in some other way, but His death on the cross requires the mention of blood. Our Lord was not only bruised and beaten, but He was put to death. His heart's blood was made to flow out of His wounds. This Person we are speaking of was God over all, blessed forever. But He stooped low to bring our humanity into union with His divinity in an amazing way. He was born at Bethlehem an infant, He grew as a child, He ripened into manhood, and lived here among us, eating and drinking, suffering and rejoicing, sleeping and laboring as men do. He really died—not figuratively, but in truth—and He was buried in the tomb of Joseph of Arimathaea. That death was the great fact contained in the words "the blood of the Lamb." We are to view Jesus as the Lamb of God's Passover. He was not only separated from others and dedicated as a memorial and consecrated for divine service; He is the Lamb that was slain. A Christ who lived but never died would not be a saving Christ. He himself said, "I am the Living One; I was dead, and behold I am alive for ever and ever!" These days some say, "Why not speak more about His life, and less about

His death?" I reply, Speak about His life as much as you want, but never apart from His death. It is by His blood that we are redeemed. "We proclaim Christ." Complete the sentence. "We proclaim Christ *crucified*," says the apostle. Yes, there is the point! It is the death of the Son of God that is the conquering weapon. If He had not "humbled Himself and become obedient to death, even death on a cross," if He had not "poured out his life unto death" and been "numbered with the transgressors," we would have had no weapon to use against the dragon prince. By "the blood of the Lamb" we understand the death of the Son of God. Hear it! Because you have sinned, Jesus died that you may be cleared from your sin. "He himself bore our sins in His body on the tree" and died that He might "redeem us from all unrighteousness." Paradoxically, this death is the vital point of the gospel. The death of Christ is the death of sin and the defeat of satan, and so it is the life of our hope and the assurance of our victory. Because He "poured out His life unto death," He "divides the spoils with the strong" (Isaiah 53).

Next, by "the blood of the Lamb" we mean *our Lord's death as a substitutionary sacrifice*. Let's be very clear here. The Spirit did not choose to say that they overcame the archenemy by the blood of Jesus, or the blood of Christ, but by the blood of the Lamb. Those words were deliberately chosen because the lamb symbolizes sacrifice. If the blood of Jesus had been shed only because of His courage for the truth, or out of simple compassion, or as an act of self-denial, it would not be especially good news for humanity, and it would have no particular power to it. A death like that might be a worthy example for martyrs, but it is not the way of salvation for guilty men and women. If you proclaim the death of the Son of God but do not show that He died as the "righteous for the unrighteous, to bring us to God," you have not proclaimed the blood of the Lamb. You must make it known that "the punishment that brought us peace was upon Him," and that "the Lord has laid on him the iniquity of us all," or you have missed the meaning of the blood of the Lamb. There is no overcoming sin without a substitutionary sacrifice. The lamb under the old law was brought by the offender to make atonement for his sin, and it took his place when it was killed. This was a picture of Christ substituting Himself for the sinner, bearing the sinner's sin and suffering in the sinner's place, and in this way satisfying the justice of God and making it possible for Him to justify the one who believes. I understand this to be the conquering weapon—the death of the Son of God as the sacrifice for sin to turn away God's anger. Sin must be punished. It is punished in Christ's death. That is our only hope.

What's more, I understand by the phrase, "The blood of the Lamb," that *our Lord's death was effective for taking away sin.* When John the Baptist first pointed to Jesus, he said, "Look, the Lamb of God, who takes away the sin of the world!" Our Lord Jesus has actually taken away sin by His death. Beloved, we are sure that He had offered an acceptable and effective sacrifice when He said, "It is finished." Either He did put away sin, or He didn't. If He didn't, how will it ever be put away? If He did, then believers are clear. Completely apart from anything that we do or are, our glorious Substitute took away our sin, just like the scapegoat carried the sin of Israel into the wilderness. If Jesus offered Himself as a substitutionary sacrifice, then God's justice is fully satisfied. God can bless the redeemed and still be just. Two thousand years ago, Jesus paid the dreadful debt of the human race, and He made a full atonement for the entire burden of sin for anyone who believes in Him. He removes the whole enormous load and throws it with one motion of His pierced hand into the depths of the sea. When Jesus died, He offered atonement, and God accepted it. In the high court of heaven there was a distinct removal of sin from the whole body that has Christ as its head. Each redeemed person individually receives for himself the great atonement by an act of personal faith, but the atonement itself was made long before.

I believe this is one of the sharp edges of the conquering weapon. We are to proclaim that the Son of God has come in the flesh and died for human sin, and that in dying He not only made it possible for God to forgive, but He secured forgiveness for all who are in Him. He did not die to make men savable, but to *save* them. He came not that sin might be put aside at some future time, but to put it away then and there by sacrificing Himself. By His death He "finished transgression, put an end to sin, atoned for wickedness, and brought in everlasting righteousness" (Daniel 9:24). Believers can know that when Jesus died they were delivered from the claims of law, and when He rose again their justification was secured. The blood of the Lamb is a real price, which powerfully ransomed them for God. The blood of the Lamb is a real cleansing, which really did purge away sin. This we believe and declare, and by this sign we conquer. Christ crucified, Christ the sacrifice for sin, Christ the powerful Redeemer of men, we will proclaim everywhere, and so put to rout the powers of darkness.

Overcoming the Enemy in Heavenly Realms

When a man gets a sword, you cannot be quite certain how he will use it. Suppose a gentleman purchases a very expensive sword with a golden hilt and an elaborate scabbard. He hangs it up in his hall and shows it to his friends. Occasionally he draws it out from the sheath and says, "Feel how sharp the edge is!" The precious blood of Jesus is not meant for us merely to admire and exhibit. We must not be content to talk about it and do nothing with it. We are to use it in the great crusade against unholiness and unrighteousness, until it can be said of us, "They overcame him by the blood of the Lamb." This precious blood is to be used for overcoming and consequently for holy warfare. We dishonor the blood if we do not use it for that purpose.

Some, I fear, use the precious blood of Christ only to soothe their consciences. They say to themselves, "He atoned for sin, so now I can relax." This is doing a severe wrong to the great sacrifice. I freely admit that the blood of Jesus does speak better things than the blood of Abel and that it cries, "Peace!" within a troubled conscience, but that is not *all* it does. A person who wants the blood of Jesus for nothing but the ordinary, selfish reason that after having been forgiven, he can say, "Take life easy; eat, drink and be merry. Listen to sermons, look forward to eternal happiness, and do nothing"—such a person blasphemes the precious blood and makes it an unholy thing. We are to use the glorious mystery of atoning blood as a weapon to conquer sin and satan. Its power is for holiness. The scripture puts it, "They overcame him by the blood of the Lamb." These saints used the teaching of atonement not as a pillow to rest on, but as a weapon to subdue their sin. Brothers and sisters, to some of us atonement by blood is our battle-axe and weapon of war, and by it we conquer in our struggle for purity and godliness—a struggle we have continued these many years. By the atoning blood we withstand corruption within and temptation without. We have a weapon that nothing can resist.

Let me show you your battle-field. Our first place of conflict is in the heavenly realm, and the second is down below on earth.

First, you who believe in the blood of Jesus have to do battle with satan *in the heavenly realms.* There you must overcome him "by the blood of the Lamb." How, you ask? Begin by regarding satan this day as already literally and truly *overcome through the death of the Lord Jesus.* Satan is already a beaten enemy. By faith grasp your Lord's victory as your own, since He triumphed on your behalf after taking on your nature. The Lord Jesus Christ went up to Calvary and there fought with the prince of darkness. He utterly defeated him and destroyed his power. He led captivity captive. He bruised the serpent's head. The victory belongs to all who are in Christ. He is the seed of the woman, and you belong to that seed. You are in Christ in reality and in your experience. When Jesus died, you then and there overcame the devil by the blood of the Lamb. Can you get a hold of this truth? Do you not know that you were circumcised in His circumcision, crucified on His cross, buried with Him in baptism, and raised with Him in His resurrection? He is your head, and you being members of His body did in Him what He did.

Come, my soul, you have conquered satan by the Lord's victory. Won't you be brave enough to fight a beaten opponent? Can't you trample down the enemy your Lord has already defeated? You have nothing to fear. Instead, say, "Thanks be to God who gives us the victory through our Lord Jesus Christ." We have overcome sin, death and hell in the person and work of our great Lord. We should be greatly encouraged by what He has already done in our name. Already "we are more than conquerors through Him who loves us." If Jesus had not overcome the enemy, certainly we never could have done it. But His personal triumph has secured ours. By faith we rise into the place of a conqueror this day. In the heavenlies we triumph, just like in every other place. We rejoice in our Lord Jesus Christ, the Redeemer of men. By Him we see satan cast out, and all the powers of evil hurled from their places of power and prominence.

This day I urge you to overcome satan in the heavenlies in another sense: *you must overcome him as the accuser.* At times you hear in your heart a voice that brings up old memories and stings your conscience; a voice which seems in the unseen realm to be a remembrance of your guilt. Listen! It is a deep, insidious voice, promising evil. Satan is repeating before the throne of justice all your former sins. Can you hear him? He begins with your childhood faults and your youthful follies. Truly a dark memory. He does not let one of your wickednesses escape notice. Things which you had forgotten he cunningly revives. He knows your secret sins, for he had a hand in most of them. He knows the resistance which you offered to the gospel, and the way in which you stifled conscience. He knows the sins of darkness, the sins of the bedroom, the crimes you committed in the inner chambers of your imagination. Since you have been a Christian he has taken note of your wickedness, and asked, in fierce sarcastic tones, "Is this a child of God? Is this an heir of heaven?" He hopes we can be found guilty of hypocrisy or apostasy.

The foul fiend points out the wanderings of our hearts, the deadness of our desires in prayer, the filthy thoughts that dropped into our minds when we were trying to worship. We have to confess that we have even tolerated doubts as to eternal truths and suspicions about the love and faithfulness of God. When the accuser is going about his evil business, he does not have to look far to find grounds for accusation and for facts to support it. Do these accusations stagger you? Do you cry, "My God, how can I face You? Because all this is true, and the sins brought to my remembrance just now are ones that I cannot deny. I have violated Your law in a thousand ways, and I cannot justify myself."

Now is your opportunity for overcoming through the blood of the Lamb. When the accuser has said his say and charged you with all your sins, do not be ashamed to step forward and say, "But I have an Advocate as well as an accuser. O Jesus, my Savior, speak for me!"

When He speaks, what does He plead but His own blood? "For all these sins I have made atonement," He says. "All these iniquities were laid on me in the day of the Lord's anger, and I have taken them away." Brothers and sisters, the blood of Jesus Christ, God's dear Son, cleanses us from all sin. Jesus has borne the penalty we deserved: He has paid for us upon the cross all our debts to the justice of God, and we are free forever, because our Surety suffered in our place. Where is the accuser now? That dragon voice is silenced by the blood of the Lamb. Nothing else can ever silence the accuser's cruel voice but the voice of the blood that tells of the infinite God accepting the sacrifice which He himself supplied on our behalf.

Justice decrees that the sinner is forgiven, because the accepted substitute has taken the sin in His own body on the tree. Come, brother or sister, the next time you have to deal with satan as an accuser in heavenly places, be careful to defend yourself with no weapon but the atonement. All comfort drawn from inward feelings or outward works will fall short. But the bleeding wounds of Jesus will plead with a full and overwhelming argument and answer all the charges. "Who will bring any charge against those whom God has chosen? It is God who justifies. Who is he that condemns? Christ Jesus, who died—more than that, who was raised to life—is at the right hand of God and is also interceding for us." Who, then, shall accuse the child of God? Every accuser will be overcome by the invincible argument of the blood of the Lamb.

What's more, the believer needs to overcome the enemy in the heavenly places when it comes to *access to God*. It may happen that when we are most focused on spending special time with God, the adversary hinders us. Our heart and our flesh cry out for God, the living God. But for one reason or another we are unable to draw near to the throne. Our heart is heavy, our sin is discouraging, our troubles are harassing us, and satanic insinuation is busy. You seem shut out from God, and the enemy triumphs over you. The world, the flesh, and the devil are nipping at your heels, but you mourn your miserable distance from God. You are like a child who cannot reach his father because a black dog barks at him from the door. What is the way to Father? If the ugly beast will not move out of the way, can we force our way in? By what weapon can we drive away the adversary so as to come to God? Isn't it written that we are "brought near by the blood"? Isn't there a "new and living way" established for us? Don't we have "confidence to enter into the Most Holy Place by the blood of Jesus"? We are sure of God's love when we see that Christ died for us. We are sure of God's favor when we see how that atonement has removed our transgressions far from us. We grasp our freedom to come to the Father, and therefore we can each say,

> "I will approach You—I will force
> My way through obstacles to You;
> I will turn to You for strength,
> Flee for consolation to You!"

Pleading the satisfaction made by the blood of the Lamb, we dare draw near to God. Watch the evil spirit make way for us! The sacred name of Jesus is one before which he flees. This name will drive away his blasphemous suggestions and foul insinuations better than anything that you can invent. The dog of hell knows the dreaded Name that makes him lie down. We must confront him with the authority and especially with the atonement of the Lamb of God. He will rage and rave all the more if we send Moses the lawgiver to silence him, for he derives his power from our violations of the law. We cannot silence him unless we bring to him the great Lord who has kept the law and made it honorable.

We next must *overcome the enemy in prayer*. We cannot always pray as we want. Do you never feel when you are in prayer as if something choked your words—and, what is worse, deadened your heart? Instead of having wings like an eagle to mount to heaven, an invisible hand clips your wings, and you cannot rise. You say within yourself, "I have no faith, and I cannot expect to succeed with God without faith. I seem to have no love. Or, if I have any, my heart lies asleep, and I cannot stir myself to plead with God. Oh, that I could come out of my prayer closet, saying, 'I have overcome, I have overcome!' But instead I groan in vain and come away unrelieved. I have been half dead, cold, and emotionless, and I cannot hope that I have prevailed with God in prayer." Whenever you are in this condition, fly to the blood of the Lamb as your most important remedy. When you make this powerful argument you will shake yourself awake, and you will prevail with God. You will feel rest in pleading it, and a sweet assurance of success at the mercy-seat. Don't hesitate for a moment. This is the way in which you should use this plea. Say, "My God, I am utterly unworthy, and I own it. But I am asking You to hear me for the honor of Your dear Son. By His agony and bloody sweat, by His cross and passion, by His precious death and burial, I implore You to hear me! O Lord, let the blood of Your Only-begotten prevail with You! Can you ignore His groans, His tears, His death, when they speak on my behalf?" If you can in this way come to terms with God, pleading on this ground, you must and will prevail. Jesus must be heard in heaven. The voice of His blood is eloquent with God. If you plead the atoning sacrifice, you must overcome through the blood of the Lamb.

Overcoming the Enemy on Earth

We have spoken of overcoming in the heavenlies, but you must also contend against the evil one in a lower sphere—ON THIS EARTH. You must first overcome in the heavenly places before the throne. When you have been triumphant with God in prayer, you will have grace to go out to serve and to defeat evil among your fellow men. How often have I personally found that the battle must first be fought above! We must overcome in order to serve. Those who know the burden of the Lord are often bowed down and would not be able to bear up at all were it not for having in secret battled with their enemy and won the day. I have been bowed down before the Lord, and in his presence I have pleaded the precious blood as the reason for obtaining help, and the help has been given. Faith, having once made sure that Jesus is hers, helps herself out of the treasury of God to all that she needs. Satan would deny her, but in the power of the blood she takes possession of covenant blessings.

You say to yourself, "I am weak, but in the Lord, my God, there is power: I take it to myself. I am hard and cold, but here is tenderness and warmth, and I appropriate it. It pleased the Father that in Jesus 'all the fullness of the Deity lives in bodily form,' and by virtue of His precious blood, I take out of that fullness what I need, and then with that help I meet the enemy and overcome him."

Satan would hinder us from getting supplies of grace with which to overcome him. But with the blood-mark on our foot we can go anywhere; with the blood-mark on our hand we dare take anything. Having access to God with confidence, we can receive with freedom whatever we need, and so we are provided against all necessities, and armed against all assaults through the atoning sacrifice. This is the fountain of supply, and the shield of security: this, indeed, is the channel through which we receive strength for victory.

We overcome the great enemy by *laying hold upon the all-sufficiency of God*, when we really grasp the power of the precious blood of Christ. So when we are victorious in the heavenlies, we come down to our homes, neighborhoods, and places of employment made "strong in the Lord and in His mighty power." Having overcome satan at the throne of grace, we see him fall from heaven like lightning, despite our feeble abilities. We speak, and God speaks with us; we long for souls, and God's great heart is yearning with us. We invite men to come, and the Lord also pleads with them to come. Spiritual power of a holy kind rests upon us to overcome the spiritual power of an evil kind which is exerted by satan, the world, and the flesh. The Lord scatters the power of the enemy, and breaks the spell which holds men captive. Through the blood of the Lamb, the weakest among us is able to "bear thirtyfold." Coming forth to serve God in the power of our victory in heaven gained by pleading the blood of the Lamb, we march together to conquer, and no power of the enemy is able to prevail against us.

On earth, among men in these lower places of conflict, saints overcome through the blood of the Lamb *by their testimony to that blood*. "They overcame by the word of their testimony." Every believer is to bear witness to the atoning sacrifice of Jesus and His power to save. He is to proclaim that truth; he is to emphasize it by earnestly believing in it himself; and he is to support it and prove it by his own experience of its power. You may not all have the gift of teacher, but you can all speak for Jesus as opportunity is given you. Our main business is to bear witness with the blood in the power of the Spirit. To this point we can all testify. You can tell all those around you, "There is life in a look at the Crucified One." You can bear witness to the power of the blood of Jesus in your own soul. If you do this, you will overcome men in many ways.

First, you will *arouse them out of apathy*. This age is more indifferent to true religion than almost any other. It is alive enough to error, but to the "faith entrusted to the saints," it turns a deaf ear. Yet I have noticed people captivated by the message of the cross who would not listen to anything else. If any truth can capture men's attention, it is the story of divine love, incarnate in the person of Jesus, bleeding and dying for guilty men. It has a fascination about it. The marvelous history of the Son of God, who loved His enemies and died for them—this will arrest our hearts. The history of the Holy One who stood in the sinners' place and so was put to shame, agony, and death—this will touch them. The sight of the bleeding Savior overcomes stubbornness and carelessness.

The truth of the blood of the Lamb prevents or *corrects error*. I do not think that by mere logic we often disprove false beliefs to any practical purpose. We may refute error rhetorically and doctrinally, but men still stick to it. But the proclamation of the precious blood, if it ever gets into the heart, drives error out of it, and sets up the throne of truth. You cannot cling to an atoning sacrifice and still delight in modern heresies. Those who deny the inspiration of scripture are sure to get rid of the cross, because it will not allow their errors. Let us go on proclaiming the truth of the great sacrifice, and it will kill the vipers of heresy. Let us lift up the cross—never mind what other people say. Maybe we have paid too much attention to them already. Let the dogs bark; it is their nature. Go on proclaiming Christ crucified. "May I never boast except in the cross of our Lord Jesus Christ, through which the world has been crucified to me, and I to the world."

We also overcome men in this way, by *softening rebellious hearts*. Men stand out against the law of God and defy the vengeance of God; but the love of God in Christ Jesus disarms them. The Holy Spirit causes men to yield through the softening influence of the cross. A bleeding Savior can make men throw down their weapons of rebellion. "If He loves me so," they say, "I cannot do other than love Him in return." We overcome men's obstinacy by the blood, poured out for many for the forgiveness of sins.

How wonderfully this same blood of the Lamb *overcomes despair*. Have you never seen a man shut up in the iron cage of despair? It has been my painful duty to talk with several such prisoners. I have seen the captive shake the iron bars, but he could not break them. He has begged us to set him free somehow, but we have been powerless. Glory to God, the blood is a universal solvent! It has dissolved the iron bars of despair, until the poor captive conscience has been able to escape. How sweet for the desponding to sing: "I believe that Jesus died for me"!

Believing *that*, all doubts and fears and despairs fly away, and the man is at peace.

There is nothing, indeed, dear friends, which the blood of the Lamb will not overcome. It *overcomes vice* and every form of sin. The world stinks with evil, like a cave which has long been the lair of filthy creatures. What can cleanse it? What but the matchless stream of the blood? Satan makes sin seem pleasurable, but the cross reveals its bitterness. If Jesus died because of sin, men begin to see that sin must be a murderous thing. Even when sin was only laid on the Savior, it made Him pour out his soul to death. It must, then, be a hideous evil to those who are actually and personally guilty of it. If God's rod made Christ sweat great drops of blood, what will His axe do when He executes the death penalty on impenitent men? Yes, we overcome the deadly sweetness and destructive pleasantness of sin by the blood of the Lamb.

This blood overcomes *the natural slowness of men to obey;* it stimulates them to holiness. If anything can make a man holy, it is a firm faith in the atoning sacrifice. When a man knows that Jesus died for him, he feels that he is not his own, but bought with a price. Jesus died for all, that those who live should no longer live for themselves but for Him who died for them and was raised again. In the atonement I see a motive equal to the greatest heroism, a motivation that will stimulate to perfect holiness. What kind of persons ought we to be, if that kind of sacrifice was offered for us? Now we are inspired into intensity of zeal and devotion. See, dear brothers, how to use the blood of the Lamb in this lower sphere while contending with evil among men.

"They Did Not Love Their Lives"

But I must close with this. It is not merely by our testimony that we use this potent truth. *We must support that testimony by our zeal and energy.* We need concentrated, consecrated energy. For the passage also says, "They did not love their lives so much as to shrink from death." We will not overcome satan if we are "nice" people who have to have an easy life and a good reputation. As long as a so-called Christian feels he must enjoy the world, the devil will have nothing to fear. Those who overcame the world in the old days were humble men and women, often poor and always despised, who were never ashamed of Christ, who only lived to tell of His love, and who died by tens of thousands rather than cease to bear testimony to the blood of the Lamb. They overcame by their heroism; their intense devotion to the cause secured the victory. Their lives to them meant nothing compared to the honor of their Lord.

If we are to win great victories we must have greater courage. Some of you hardly dare to speak about the blood of Christ anywhere but in religious company—and hardly even there. You blend right in. You love yourselves too much to get into trouble through your religion. Surely you cannot belong to that noble band that did not love their lives so much as to shrink from death! Many dare not proclaim the truth of God these days because they would be thought narrow and bigoted, and this would be too upsetting. They call us fools. It is very likely we are. But we are not ashamed to be fools for Christ and His truth. We believe in the blood of the Lamb, despite any so-called "discovery of science." We will never give up the truth of Christ's atoning sacrifice to please modern culture. What little reputation we have is as dear to us as another man's character is to him; but we will cheerfully let it go in this struggle for the central truth of revelation. It will be sweet to be forgotten and lost sight of, or to be vilified and abused, if the faith in Christ and Him crucified can not only survive but thrive. This much we are resolved on, we will be true to our convictions about the sacrifice of Jesus. If we give this up, what is left?

God will not do anything by us if we are false to the cross. He uses people who do not spare their reputations when they are called for in defense of truth. Oh, to be at a white heat! Oh, to flame with zeal for Jesus! Brothers and sisters, hold to the true faith, and say, "As for the respect of men, I can readily forfeit it; but as for the truth of God, that I can never give up." This is the day for men to be men, because sadly, most are soft, mollusk-like creatures. Now we need backbones as well as heads. To believe the truth concerning the Lamb of God, and truly to believe it, is essential to an overcoming life. Oh, for courage, faithfulness, determination, self-denial, willingness to be made nothing for Christ! May God give us the grace to be faithful witnesses to the blood of the Lamb in the midst of this ungodly world!

As for those of you who are not saved, your hope lies in the blood of the Lamb.

> "Come, guilty souls, and flee away,
> Like doves, to Jesus' wounds."

The atoning sacrifice, which is our glory, is your salvation. Trust in him whom God has set forth to be the sacrifice for sin. Begin with this, and you are saved. Every good and holy thing which goes with salvation will follow after; but now, this day, I pray you receive a current salvation through the blood of the Lamb. "Whoever believes in the Son has eternal life."